I0031130

Leadership, Sales and Spirituality: A Harmonious Blueprint for Business Success

Jan Jacobus Kriel

Published by Jan Jacobus Kriel, 2023.

While every precaution has been taken in the preparation of this book, the publisher assumes no responsibility for errors or omissions, or for damages resulting from the use of the information contained herein.

LEADERSHIP, SALES AND SPIRITUALITY: A HARMONIOUS BLUEPRINT FOR BUSINESS SUCCESS

First edition. November 7, 2023.

Copyright © 2023 Jan Jacobus Kriel.

ISBN: 978-0796124340

Written by Jan Jacobus Kriel.

Table of Contents

About the Author

This book provides an in-depth exploration of leadership, sales, and spirituality and their interconnectedness in creating a thriving and successful business. Readers will gain practical insights and strategies to enhance their leadership skills, excel in sales, and infuse spirituality into their business practices to achieve holistic growth and fulfillment.

Chapter 1: Introduction

The Triad of Success: Leadership, Sales, and Spirituality

In the complex tapestry of the business world, three threads stand out as critical components of success: leadership, sales, and spirituality. This chapter introduces you to the interwoven nature of these elements and the profound impact they have on holistic business growth.

The Anatomy of Success

Success in business is often likened to a well-tuned orchestra, where each instrument represents a crucial aspect of the symphony. In this analogy, leadership, sales, and spirituality are the conductor, the musicians, and the soul of the music, respectively. To understand how this symphony works, we must delve into the essence of each component.

Leadership: The Conductor

At the heart of any successful business lies effective leadership. Leaders are the visionary conductors who guide the orchestra of employees towards a common goal. They set the tone, establish the tempo, and ensure harmony among team members. Leadership isn't just about making decisions; it's about inspiring and motivating others to achieve greatness.

Sales: The Musicians

Sales are the musicians who play the melodies of revenue and growth. They are the frontline warriors who engage with customers, build relationships, and close deals. Effective salespeople understand the intricacies of their instruments, such as persuasion, negotiation, and empathy, to create beautiful symphonies of profit and success.

Spirituality: The Soul of the Music

Now, let's introduce an often overlooked but profoundly impactful element: spirituality. In a business context, spirituality is not about religious beliefs but about core values, purpose, and the deeper meaning behind our actions. It's the soul of the music that adds depth and resonance to the symphony. When individuals and organizations infuse their work with spirituality, they tap into a wellspring of inspiration, resilience, and ethical behavior.

Holistic Business Growth

As we explore the triad of leadership, sales, and spirituality, it becomes evident that holistic business growth is not solely about profit margins and market share. It's about nurturing an environment where these three components harmonize to create something greater than the sum of their parts.

People-Centric Leadership: Holistic growth begins with leadership that prioritizes people. Leaders who understand their team's needs and aspirations can inspire loyalty, creativity, and dedication. Authentic leaders foster a sense of belonging and purpose, which drives individuals to go above and beyond.

Sales as a Service: Successful salespeople don't just sell products; they provide solutions and value. A holistic approach to sales involves genuinely understanding customer needs and concerns. When salespeople approach their work with empathy and integrity, they forge lasting relationships that lead to sustainable growth.

Spiritual Alignment: Infusing spirituality into business means aligning your organization's values with a higher purpose. This alignment guides decision-making, fosters ethical behavior, and encourages employees to find meaning in their work. It creates a workplace where individuals are not just cogs in a machine but integral contributors to a larger vision.

The Power of Integration

Imagine a business where leaders inspire with purpose, salespeople connect on a deep level with customers, and everyone works with a sense of shared values. This is the power of integration—where leadership, sales, and spirituality converge to create a symphony of success.

Throughout this book, we will explore each of these components in detail, offering insights, strategies, and practical examples to help you unlock their full potential. Whether you're a seasoned executive, an aspiring entrepreneur, or someone simply seeking to elevate your career and personal growth, the triad of leadership, sales, and spirituality will serve as your guide to achieving holistic business success. Together, we will uncover the transformative potential of this triad and discover how it can elevate not only your business but your life as well.

Part 1: Leadership
Chapter 2: The Essence of Leadership

Leadership is the cornerstone of any successful organization. It's the driving force that shapes the vision, culture, and direction of a business. In the context of business success, leadership can be defined as the art and science of inspiring, guiding, and influencing individuals or teams to achieve common goals and objectives effectively and ethically. It encompasses a multifaceted set of skills, behaviors, and attributes that enable individuals to steer their organizations toward prosperity and fulfillment.

The Evolution of Leadership

Leadership, as a concept, has evolved significantly over time. It's a reflection of the changing needs and challenges of society and the business world. Understanding the evolving nature of leadership is crucial to adapt to the demands of the modern corporate landscape.

1. Traditional Leadership (Pre-20th Century)

In earlier centuries, leadership was often associated with authority and hierarchy. Leaders were typically those in positions of power, such as monarchs, military commanders, or heads of aristocratic families. Leadership was often autocratic, where decisions were made unilaterally, and subordinates were expected to follow orders without question.

2. Transactional Leadership (20th Century)

The industrial revolution and the growth of large corporations in the 20th century brought about a shift in leadership styles. Transactional leadership emerged as a dominant model, focusing on exchanges between leaders and followers. Leaders offered rewards or punishments to motivate employees to achieve specific goals. This approach emphasized compliance and efficiency.

3. Transformational Leadership (Late 20th Century)

As organizations became more complex and competitive, a new leadership paradigm emerged - transformational leadership. This style centers on inspiring and motivating individuals to go beyond their self-interest for the collective good. Transformational leaders encourage creativity, innovation, and personal development. They lead by example, promote shared values, and create a vision that resonates with their teams.

4. Servant Leadership (Late 20th Century to Present)

Servant leadership emphasizes leaders' role as servants first. Leaders prioritize the needs of their team members, focusing on their well-being, development, and success. By serving their teams, servant leaders create a culture of trust and collaboration, which, in turn, drives organizational success.

5. Adaptive Leadership (21st Century)

In the fast-paced, uncertain, and globalized world of the 21st century, adaptive leadership has gained prominence. Adaptive leaders are flexible and can navigate complex challenges by encouraging continuous learning and adaptability within their organizations. They thrive in ambiguity and guide their teams through change and uncertainty.

6. Ethical Leadership (Ongoing Emphasis)

Today, there's a growing emphasis on ethical leadership. Ethical leaders prioritize moral and principled decision-making, aligning their actions with the organization's values and societal expectations. They hold themselves accountable for their choices and set an example for ethical behavior throughout the organization.

Conclusion: The Ever-Evolving Role of Leadership

Leadership in the context of business success is not a one-size-fits-all concept. It has evolved from traditional autocratic models to more adaptive, inclusive, and ethical approaches. In the dynamic landscape of the modern business world, successful leaders must be agile, ethical, and capable of inspiring and empowering their teams.

Understanding this evolving nature of leadership is essential for contemporary leaders and aspiring ones. It underscores the need for a versatile leadership style that can adapt to changing circumstances while staying true to core values and ethics. Leadership in today's context is not merely about achieving short-term goals but about fostering a culture of growth, innovation, and sustainability for long-term success.

The Wisdom of Wolves : Leadership, an art that has been studied and refined for centuries, finds its roots in the most unlikely of places - the natural world. One of the most fascinating sources of inspiration for leadership is the wisdom of wolves. These magnificent creatures have a lot to teach us about effective teamwork, communication, and hierarchy. In this exploration, we'll dive deep into the world of wolf packs and uncover the valuable insights they offer to leaders in the modern business landscape.

Pack Dynamics: The Essence of Teamwork

Wolves are social animals known for their remarkable pack dynamics. At the core of their society lies the concept of teamwork, which is the bedrock of successful leadership in any organization. Here's how the wisdom of wolves can inspire effective teamwork:

1. Mutual Interdependence: Wolves depend on each other for survival. They work together to hunt, protect their territory, and care for their young. In a business context, leaders can learn that every member of the team plays a crucial role, and their success is interlinked. Encouraging mutual interdependence among team members fosters collaboration and a sense of belonging.

2. Clear Roles and Responsibilities: Wolf packs have clearly defined roles within the group. The alpha pair leads, while other members have specific duties, such as hunting or caring for the pups. This clear division of labor ensures that everyone contributes to the pack's success. In organizations, leaders can benefit from assigning roles and responsibilities based on individual strengths and expertise.

3. Effective Communication: Wolves communicate effectively through vocalizations, body language, and scent marking. Their communication is precise, allowing them to coordinate hunts and maintain social order. Leaders can draw inspiration from this by emphasizing the importance of open, honest, and clear communication within their teams.

Hierarchy and Leadership: Lessons from the Alpha

The alpha wolf, often seen as the leader of the pack, provides profound insights into leadership. While the concept of a dominant leader might seem at odds with modern leadership philosophies, there are valuable takeaways:

1. Leading with Purpose: The alpha's role is not about dominance for its sake but about ensuring the pack's survival. In the business world, leaders can align their vision with a larger purpose, guiding their teams toward a shared goal that transcends individual ambitions.

2. Decision-Making Authority: The alpha wolf is responsible for making critical decisions, such as when to hunt and where to establish territory. While modern leadership advocates for collaborative decision-making, there are times when leaders must take charge and make tough choices for the greater good.

3. Leading by Example: The alpha leads by example, demonstrating behaviors that set the tone for the entire pack. Leaders can emulate this by modeling the values and work ethic they expect from their teams. Leading by example creates a culture of accountability and integrity.

Adaptability and Resilience

Wolves are adaptable creatures, thriving in diverse environments, from arctic tundras to forests. This adaptability teaches us that effective leaders must be flexible and able to navigate changing circumstances. In the modern business world, adaptability is key to surviving and thriving amidst rapid technological advancements, market shifts, and global challenges.

Additionally, wolves' resilience in the face of adversity is a powerful lesson for leaders. They persevere through harsh winters and lean times, showing that resilience is a quality that leaders and teams should cultivate to weather challenges and emerge stronger.

Inclusivity and Social Bonds

Wolves exhibit strong social bonds within their packs. They prioritize the welfare of their fellow pack members and ensure that everyone is cared for. This sense of inclusivity underscores the importance of fostering a culture of inclusion and belonging in organizations. Effective leaders recognize the value of diverse perspectives and create an environment where every team member feels valued and supported.

Conclusion: Lessons from Nature's Classroom

The wisdom of wolves offers a rich tapestry of lessons for leadership in the modern business world. From teamwork and communication to hierarchy, adaptability, and inclusivity, wolves exemplify qualities and behaviors that can guide leaders toward success.

Leaders who draw inspiration from nature's classroom, as exemplified by wolf packs, can create organizations that are not only efficient and productive but also nurturing and purpose-driven. By embracing these timeless lessons, leaders can cultivate a culture of collaboration, resilience, and inclusivity that will empower their teams to thrive in an ever-evolving business landscape. The wisdom of wolves reminds us that the natural world has much to teach us about being effective and compassionate leaders.

Chapter 3: Leadership Qualities

The Attributes of Exceptional Leaders : Exceptional leaders are the cornerstone of successful organizations. They possess a unique set of qualities that set them apart and allow them to inspire, guide, and drive their teams toward greatness. In this exploration, we will delve deep into the essential qualities that distinguish exceptional leaders, including vision, decisiveness, adaptability, and courage. Using real-world examples, we will illustrate the profound impact these attributes have on leadership success.

1. Vision: Painting a Compelling Picture of the Future

Vision is the North Star that guides exceptional leaders. It's the ability to see a clear, compelling, and inspiring picture of the future and communicate that vision to their teams. Visionary leaders not only understand the present challenges and opportunities but also have a keen sense of where their organization should be heading.

Steve Jobs: The Visionary Behind Apple

Steve Jobs, the co-founder of Apple Inc., is a shining example of a leader with an unwavering vision. He envisioned a world where technology seamlessly integrated into our daily lives. His vision led to the creation of groundbreaking products like the iPhone and iPad, transforming Apple into one of the world's most influential and profitable companies.

Jobs' ability to inspire his teams with his vision transcended his own lifetime. Apple continues to innovate based on the foundation he laid, demonstrating the enduring impact of a visionary leader.

2. Decisiveness: Making Informed and Timely Choices

Decisiveness is the ability to make informed and timely decisions, even in the face of uncertainty and complexity. Exceptional leaders possess the confidence and analytical skills to assess options, weigh risks, and choose a course of action, inspiring confidence and trust among their teams.

Indra Nooyi: Decisiveness at PepsiCo

Indra Nooyi, the former CEO of PepsiCo, demonstrated exceptional decisiveness during her tenure. Facing a changing market landscape, she made pivotal decisions, such as diversifying the product portfolio to include healthier options and expanding into international markets.

Nooyi's bold and decisive moves positioned PepsiCo for long-term growth and sustainability. Her leadership exemplified how well-informed and timely decisions can transform a company's trajectory.

3. Adaptability: Navigating Change with Agility

Adaptability is the capacity to embrace change and uncertainty with agility. Exceptional leaders recognize that the business landscape is in constant flux and understand the need to pivot, evolve, and innovate in response to new challenges and opportunities.

Satya Nadella: Leading Microsoft's Transformation

Satya Nadella, the CEO of Microsoft, exemplifies adaptability in leadership. Upon assuming the role in 2014, he recognized the need to shift Microsoft's focus from a traditional software company to a cloud-centric organization. This strategic pivot involved a cultural shift and embracing new technologies and business models.

Under Nadella's leadership, Microsoft's market value surged, showcasing the power of adaptability in navigating significant industry transformations.

4. Courage: Embracing Risk and Confronting Challenges

Courage is the ability to embrace risk, confront challenges, and persevere in the face of adversity. Exceptional leaders are not deterred by fear of failure but are motivated by the potential for growth and innovation that comes from taking calculated risks.

Oprah Winfrey: Courage in Media and Entertainment

Oprah Winfrey, a media mogul and philanthropist, embodies courage in leadership. Throughout her career, she took bold steps, such as launching "The Oprah Winfrey Show" and establishing her media empire. She tackled sensitive and challenging topics fearlessly, inspiring conversations and change.

Winfrey's courage to speak out on important issues and her willingness to take risks in her career have made her an iconic figure in media and entertainment.

5. Empathy: Understanding and Connecting with Others

Empathy is the ability to understand and connect with others on an emotional level. Exceptional leaders are attuned to the needs, feelings, and perspectives of their team members. They create a supportive and inclusive environment that fosters collaboration and trust.

Bill Gates: Empathy in Philanthropy

Bill Gates, co-founder of Microsoft and a renowned philanthropist, demonstrates empathy in his leadership. Through the Bill & Melinda Gates Foundation, he has channeled his wealth and influence to address global health and education issues.

Gates' empathy for the less fortunate and his commitment to improving lives around the world exemplify how empathy can drive impactful leadership.

6. Integrity: Upholding Ethical Principles

Integrity is the commitment to ethical principles and moral values. Exceptional leaders lead with integrity, ensuring that their actions align with their organization's values and ethical standards. They inspire trust, credibility, and transparency among their teams.

Warren Buffett: Integrity in Investing

Warren Buffett, one of the world's most successful investors and the chairman and CEO of Berkshire Hathaway, is a paragon of integrity in leadership. He adheres to a strict ethical code in his investment decisions and has consistently emphasized the importance of trust and reputation in business.

Buffett's unwavering commitment to integrity has earned him the respect and trust of investors and stakeholders alike.

Conclusion: The Blueprint for Exceptional Leadership

Exceptional leaders are not born; they are forged through a combination, vision and the ability take control and forcing themselves to never stop learning and staying true to their core values, without exception.

Resilience and Perseverance :. In the ever-evolving landscape of leadership, two qualities stand as unwavering pillars: resilience and perseverance. These qualities enable leaders to face adversity and setbacks with unwavering determination and to emerge stronger from the crucible of challenges. In this exploration, we will delve into the critical importance of resilience and perseverance in leadership, sharing stories of leaders who have faced remarkable adversity while remaining steadfast in their pursuit of their vision.

1. Resilience: Bouncing Back from Adversity

Resilience is the ability to bounce back from adversity, to withstand setbacks and challenges, and to emerge even stronger. In the realm of leadership, resilience is the armor that shields leaders from the inevitable storms they encounter on their journey.

Story 1: Nelson Mandela's Triumph Over Apartheid

Nelson Mandela, the iconic leader of South Africa's anti-apartheid movement, epitomizes resilience in leadership. For 27 years, Mandela endured imprisonment under harsh conditions, yet he never wavered in his commitment to ending apartheid and establishing a democratic, racially inclusive South Africa.

Upon his release, Mandela demonstrated remarkable resilience by fostering reconciliation and unity in a divided nation. His unwavering resolve in the face of adversity laid the foundation for a new South Africa, earning him the reverence of the world.

Story 2: Elon Musk's Tenacity in Space Exploration

Elon Musk, the visionary founder of SpaceX, showcases resilience in the modern corporate world. SpaceX faced multiple failures and near-bankruptcy during its early years. Despite multiple rocket launch failures and setbacks, Musk remained resolute in his goal of reducing space transportation costs and making humanity a multi-planetary species.

SpaceX eventually achieved remarkable successes, including the first privately-funded spacecraft to reach orbit and the development of reusable rockets. Musk's resilience in the face of adversity played a pivotal role in the company's achievements and its role in shaping the future of space exploration.

2. Perseverance: The Art of Relentless Pursuit

Perseverance is the unwavering commitment to a goal, the willingness to endure hardship and setbacks without surrender. Exceptional leaders recognize that the path to success is often paved with obstacles, and it's their perseverance that fuels their progress.

Story 1: Thomas Edison's Illuminating Perseverance

Thomas Edison, one of history's greatest inventors, epitomizes perseverance. He endured thousands of failures while developing the incandescent light bulb. Each setback, in his words, was merely a discovery of another way not to invent the light bulb. His relentless pursuit of innovation ultimately led to the invention of the practical electric light bulb, changing the course of history.

Edison's unwavering perseverance serves as a beacon for leaders, reminding them that success often requires tenacity and an unyielding commitment to their vision.

Story 2: Jeff Bezos' Long-Term Vision for Amazon

Jeff Bezos, the founder of Amazon, demonstrates extraordinary perseverance in building one of the world's largest e-commerce and technology companies. In Amazon's early years, it faced skepticism, financial challenges, and questions about its viability.

Bezos, however, remained steadfast in his long-term vision for the company. He prioritized customer satisfaction, invested heavily in innovation, and expanded Amazon's services. Over the years, his perseverance transformed Amazon into a global retail and technology giant.

The Symbiosis of Resilience and Perseverance

Resilience and perseverance are not isolated qualities; they coexist and complement each other in effective leadership.

1. Resilience Fuels Perseverance: Resilience equips leaders with the emotional fortitude needed to weather setbacks and failures. It provides the strength to stand up after a fall and keep moving forward, enabling leaders to persevere through adversity.

2. Perseverance Sustains Resilience: Perseverance, on the other hand, fuels the determination to continue the journey. It propels leaders forward, allowing them to learn from setbacks, adapt to challenges, and grow stronger over time.

3. Together, They Foster Growth: The symbiosis of resilience and perseverance fosters growth, both for the leader and the organization. Leaders who possess these qualities create a culture that values resilience and encourages perseverance among team members.

Leading by Example: Resilience and Perseverance in Action

Exceptional leaders lead by example, embodying resilience and perseverance in their actions, which, in turn, inspire and empower their teams.

Story 1: Malala Yousafzai's Unyielding Commitment to Education

Malala Yousafzai, the youngest Nobel Prize laureate, demonstrated exceptional resilience and perseverance in advocating for girls' education in Pakistan. Despite being shot by the Taliban and facing numerous threats, she continued to speak out for the right to education for all.

Malala's unyielding commitment and courage inspire millions worldwide and exemplify how resilience and perseverance can spark transformative change.

Story 2: Howard Schultz's Starbucks Journey

Howard Schultz, the former CEO and chairman of Starbucks, embodies these qualities in the world of business. Schultz faced multiple challenges in turning Starbucks into the global coffeehouse chain it is today. His journey included overcoming financial struggles, resistance from investors, and competition.

Schultz's unwavering belief in the Starbucks experience and his determination to provide a "third place" for people beyond home and work led to the company's resurgence. His story underscores how resilience and perseverance can turn a struggling company into an iconic brand.

The Role of Failure in Resilience and Perseverance

Failure is an inevitable part of any leadership journey. Exceptional leaders view failure not as a roadblock but as a stepping stone toward growth and innovation. They understand that it's often through failure that they learn the most valuable lessons.

1. **Failure as a Learning Opportunity**: Resilient leaders view failure as an opportunity to learn, adapt, and improve. They embrace the lessons that failure provides, leveraging them to make informed decisions and drive progress.

2. **Persistence in the Face of Failure**: Persevering leaders do not let failure deter them. They understand that setbacks are temporary, and with continued effort, they can overcome challenges and achieve their goals.

3. **Transforming Failure into Success**: Exceptional leaders, like Thomas Edison, recognize that each failure brings them one step closer to success. By refining their approach and persevering, they eventually achieve their objectives.

Conclusion: The Indomitable Spirit of Resilient Perseverance

In the tapestry of leadership, resilience and perseverance stand as threads of indomitable spirit. Exceptional leaders harness these qualities to weather storms, surmount obstacles, and drive their organizations toward success

Empathy and Connection: In the realm of leadership, success is not solely determined by strategic prowess or decision-making acumen. Rather, it hinges on the ability to connect with and understand the emotions and perspectives of others. Empathy and emotional intelligence serve as the bedrock upon which exceptional leaders build strong interpersonal connections within their teams. In this exploration, we will illuminate the significance of empathy and emotional intelligence in effective leadership, drawing inspiration from the social bonds of wolf packs to offer insights into fostering these crucial qualities within teams.

1. The Significance of Empathy in Leadership

Empathy is the capacity to understand and share the feelings of others. It is the ability to step into someone else's shoes, to see the world from their perspective, and to respond with compassion and understanding. In the world of leadership, empathy is the bridge that connects leaders to their teams and paves the way for trust, collaboration, and motivation.

Empathy Fosters Trust: Empathetic leaders create an environment in which team members feel heard and valued. When employees believe their leaders genuinely care about their well-being and concerns, trust flourishes.

Empathy Enhances Communication: Understanding the emotions and perspectives of others allows leaders to communicate more effectively. They can tailor their messages to resonate with their audience and address their unique needs.

Empathy Promotes Inclusivity: Empathetic leaders are more likely to value diversity and inclusivity. They recognize the importance of considering different viewpoints and fostering an inclusive culture where every team member feels respected and included.

Story 1: Abraham Lincoln's Empathy in Leadership

Abraham Lincoln, the 16th President of the United States, demonstrated exceptional empathy during a period of great turmoil—the American Civil War. His empathetic leadership style, characterized by listening to the concerns of soldiers and citizens alike, played a crucial role in unifying a divided nation.

Lincoln's ability to connect with the emotions and struggles of those around him earned him the trust and support of many, making him one of the most revered leaders in American history.

2. Emotional Intelligence: The Art of Self-Awareness and Regulation

Emotional intelligence (EI) extends beyond empathy to encompass a broader spectrum of emotional awareness and regulation. Leaders with high EI possess the ability to recognize and manage their own emotions effectively while also understanding and influencing the emotions of others.

Self-Awareness: EI begins with self-awareness—a deep understanding of one's own emotions, strengths, and weaknesses. Leaders who are self-aware are better equipped to handle challenging situations and make informed decisions.

Self-Regulation: Leaders with strong EI can regulate their emotions, avoiding impulsive reactions and maintaining composure under pressure. This skill is vital in maintaining a calm and steady presence within the team.

Empathy: Empathy, a key component of EI, allows leaders to connect with the emotions of others. Leaders with high EI can accurately gauge the feelings of team members and respond in a supportive and understanding manner.

Story 2: Sundar Pichai's Emotional Intelligence at Google

Sundar Pichai, the CEO of Google and Alphabet Inc., exemplifies emotional intelligence in leadership. He navigated Google through various challenges, such as ethical dilemmas and employee protests. Pichai's ability to listen to employee concerns, address their needs, and regulate his own emotions in high-pressure situations has contributed to his success as a leader.

Under Pichai's leadership, Google has maintained its position as a global tech leader while fostering a culture of openness and inclusion.

3. Wolf Packs and the Power of Social Bonds

Wolves, as social animals, provide a captivating model of social bonds and cooperation within a pack. They rely on one another for survival and success. Observing wolf pack dynamics reveals valuable insights into the importance of empathy, emotional intelligence, and strong interpersonal connections in leadership.

Strong Social Bonds: Wolf packs thrive on strong social bonds. These bonds are built on trust, cooperation, and mutual support. In leadership, strong interpersonal connections foster collaboration, teamwork, and a sense of belonging.

Communication: Wolves communicate not only through vocalizations but also through body language and scent marking. Effective communication is essential for coordinating group activities and maintaining social order. Leaders can learn from this and emphasize clear, multi-faceted communication within their teams.

Story 3: Jane Goodall's Empathy for Chimpanzees

While not wolves, Jane Goodall's work with chimpanzees showcases the power of empathy and emotional intelligence in understanding and connecting with other species. Her ability to empathize with chimpanzees allowed her to observe and document their behavior in a way that transformed our understanding of these animals.

Goodall's pioneering research demonstrated the importance of empathy, patience, and emotional intelligence in the scientific field.

Her work continues to inspire empathy and understanding for chimpanzees and other wildlife.

Fostering Empathy and Emotional Intelligence in Teams

Exceptional leaders actively foster empathy and emotional intelligence within their teams. Here are strategies to cultivate these qualities:

Lead by Example: Demonstrate empathy and emotional intelligence in your interactions with team members. Your behavior sets the tone for the organization.

Encourage Open Communication: Create an environment where team members feel comfortable expressing their thoughts and emotions. Encourage open dialogue and active listening.

Provide Emotional Support: Offer support and resources to help team members manage their emotional well-being. This can include mental health programs, coaching, or access to counseling services.

Promote Diversity and Inclusivity: Embrace diversity and inclusivity within the organization. Different perspectives and backgrounds contribute to a richer tapestry of experiences and ideas.

Invest in Emotional Intelligence Training: Provide training and resources to enhance emotional intelligence within the organization. This can include workshops, coaching, and resources for personal development.

Conclusion: The Heart-Centered Leadership

In the complex landscape of leadership, empathy and emotional intelligence serve as compasses, guiding leaders toward creating strong interpersonal connections within their teams. By recognizing the significance of these qualities and drawing inspiration from the social bonds of wolf packs, leaders can foster trust, cooperation, and a sense of belonging that propels their organizations toward success. Empathy and emotional intelligence, when cultivated and applied with intention, transform leaders into heart-centered stewards of their teams and organizations, driving positive change and lasting impact.

Effective Communication : Effective communication is the cornerstone of successful leadership. It is the art of conveying thoughts, ideas, and emotions in a manner that fosters understanding, trust, and collaboration within a team or organization. In this exploration, we will delve deep into the intricacies of effective communication in leadership, exploring various techniques, both verbal and non-verbal, that leaders can employ to promote collaboration and trust.

1. The Foundation of Effective Communication

Before delving into specific techniques, it's essential to understand the core principles that underpin effective communication in leadership:

Clarity: Clear and concise communication ensures that the intended message is easily understood. Ambiguity can lead to confusion and misunderstandings.

Active Listening: Effective communication is a two-way process that involves active listening. Leaders should listen attentively to their team members, showing that their perspectives are valued.

Empathy: Leaders who empathize with their team members can better understand their needs and concerns, creating a more supportive and collaborative environment.

Transparency: Open and honest communication builds trust. Leaders should be transparent about goals, challenges, and decisions.

Adaptability: Effective communicators adapt their communication style to their audience, ensuring that the message resonates with the recipient.

2. Verbal Communication Techniques

i. Clarity and Conciseness: Leaders should strive for clarity and conciseness in their verbal communication. Avoiding jargon and unnecessary complexity ensures that the message is easily understood. Use concrete examples and straightforward language to convey ideas.

ii. Active Listening: Active listening involves giving full attention to the speaker, asking clarifying questions, and providing feedback.

This technique demonstrates respect for the speaker's perspective and encourages open dialogue.

iii. Asking Powerful Questions: Leaders can foster productive discussions by asking open-ended questions that encourage critical thinking and reflection. These questions stimulate deeper conversations and insights.

iv. Storytelling: Stories have the power to captivate and inspire. Leaders can use storytelling to convey important messages, share experiences, and create a connection with their audience.

v. Feedback: Providing constructive feedback is a crucial aspect of effective communication. Leaders should offer feedback that is specific, actionable, and delivered in a supportive manner.

3. Non-Verbal Communication Techniques

Non-verbal communication is equally important in conveying messages and building trust. Leaders should pay attention to their body language, facial expressions, and gestures.

i. Body Language: Maintaining open and confident body language conveys approachability and confidence. Avoiding defensive postures, such as crossed arms, can signal receptivity.

ii. Eye Contact: Making appropriate eye contact while speaking and listening demonstrates engagement and attentiveness. It conveys that the person is genuinely interested in the conversation.

iii. Facial Expressions: Leaders should be mindful of their facial expressions, as they often reveal emotions and attitudes. Smiles and positive expressions can create a welcoming atmosphere.

iv. Gestures: Using appropriate gestures can enhance verbal communication. Gestures should complement the spoken words and convey enthusiasm or emphasis.

v. Tone of Voice: The tone of voice can significantly impact the message's meaning. Leaders should strive for a confident and steady tone that matches the content of their message.

4. Digital Communication Techniques

In today's digital age, leaders often communicate through various digital channels, such as email, video conferencing, and instant messaging. Effectively navigating digital communication is essential for leadership success.

i. **Clarity in Written Communication**: In written communication, leaders should maintain clarity and avoid misunderstandings by proofreading emails and documents for clarity and conciseness.

ii. **Virtual Presence**: In virtual meetings, leaders should maintain a strong virtual presence by being engaged, participating actively, and ensuring that technology runs smoothly.

iii. **Video Communication**: In video meetings, leaders should pay attention to their appearance, background, and lighting to create a professional and engaging atmosphere.

iv. **Timeliness**: Responding promptly to digital messages and requests demonstrates respect for others' time and priorities.

5. Tailoring Communication to the Audience

Effective leaders understand that different audiences require different communication approaches. They adapt their communication style to connect with diverse groups, including team members, stakeholders, and clients.

i. **Understanding Audience Needs**: Leaders should consider the needs, expectations, and preferences of their audience. What information is most relevant to them? What communication style will resonate with them?

ii. **Flexibility**: Leaders should be flexible in their communication style, switching between formal and informal communication as needed. Flexibility helps bridge gaps and fosters rapport.

iii. **Empathetic Communication**: Empathetic leaders can connect with their audience on a deeper level by acknowledging their emotions and concerns. This approach builds trust and understanding.

iv. Cultural Sensitivity: In a globalized world, leaders should be culturally sensitive in their communication. They should respect cultural norms, customs, and communication preferences.

6. Building Trust Through Communication

Building trust is a fundamental aspect of effective leadership, and communication plays a pivotal role in this process. Trust is the foundation upon which strong teams and organizations are built.

Consistency: Leaders should consistently communicate their values, vision, and expectations. Consistency creates predictability and reliability, enhancing trust.

Transparency: Open and honest communication, even in difficult situations, demonstrates integrity and builds trust. Leaders should share information about decisions, challenges, and goals.

Authenticity and Integrity: Authentic leadership is a concept that has gained increasing attention in recent years as a response to the need for genuine and ethical leadership in today's complex and dynamic business environment. At its core, authentic leadership emphasizes the importance of leaders being true to themselves and their values, while also demonstrating integrity in their decision-making processes. In this exploration, we will delve deep into the concept of authentic leadership and its paramount importance in fostering trust, credibility, and ethical decision-making within organizations.

1. Understanding Authentic Leadership

Authentic leadership is a leadership style that places a high value on genuineness, self-awareness, and ethical behavior. Authentic leaders are characterized by their ability to:

i. Self-reflect: Authentic leaders engage in self-reflection to understand their values, beliefs, and principles. They are in touch with their true selves and are not afraid to be vulnerable.

ii. Demonstrate Transparency: They are transparent in their actions and decisions, sharing information openly and honestly with their team members and stakeholders.

iii. Build Trust: Authentic leaders build trust by consistently aligning their words with their actions. Their credibility is grounded in their authenticity.

iv. Foster a Positive Work Environment: They create a positive and inclusive work environment where team members feel valued and empowered to be their authentic selves.

v. Embrace Adversity: Authentic leaders are not afraid to confront challenges and adversity head-on, relying on their values to guide them through difficult situations.

2. The Role of Integrity in Authentic Leadership

At the heart of authentic leadership lies **integrity**, a fundamental ethical principle that serves as the bedrock of this leadership style. Integrity is the quality of being honest and having strong moral principles. It involves doing what is right even when it is difficult or inconvenient. For authentic leaders, integrity is not negotiable; it is the cornerstone of their decision-making process.

i. Upholding Ethical Standards: Authentic leaders adhere to the highest ethical standards in all their actions and decisions. They refuse to compromise their values for short-term gains.

ii. Trustworthiness: Integrity breeds trust. Authentic leaders are trusted because their team members and stakeholders know they will always act with honesty and fairness.

iii. Accountability: Authentic leaders hold themselves accountable for their actions and decisions. They take responsibility for both their successes and their mistakes.

iv. Transparency: Integrity is closely linked to transparency. Authentic leaders are transparent in their communication, ensuring that information is shared openly and honestly.

v. Ethical Decision-Making: Authentic leaders prioritize ethical decision-making. They consider the broader impact of their choices on their team, organization, and society as a whole.

3. Authentic Leadership in Action

To illustrate the concept of authentic leadership and the paramount importance of integrity in decision-making, we can explore real-world examples of leaders who have embodied these principles.

i. Nelson Mandela: The Epitome of Authentic Leadership

Nelson Mandela, the iconic leader of the anti-apartheid movement in South Africa and the country's first black president, exemplified authentic leadership. Throughout his life, Mandela remained true to his values of equality, justice, and reconciliation.

Integrity in Action: Mandela's unwavering commitment to these values is most evident during his time in prison. Despite facing incredible adversity, he refused to compromise his principles or seek revenge against his oppressors. His decision to pursue reconciliation rather than retribution was a testament to his integrity.

ii. Warren Buffett: The Sage of Ethical Investing

Warren Buffett, one of the world's most successful investors, is often cited as a model of authentic leadership in the business world. His investment philosophy is rooted in integrity, ethics, and a long-term perspective.

Integrity in Action: Buffett's approach to decision-making is guided by his principles of honesty and fairness. He prioritizes the interests of shareholders and refuses to engage in unethical or speculative practices. His commitment to ethical investing has earned him the trust of investors and stakeholders worldwide.

iii. Malala Yousafzai: Championing Education and Equality

Malala Yousafzai, the youngest Nobel Prize laureate, has become a global symbol of the fight for girls' education. Her leadership style is deeply rooted in authenticity and integrity.

Integrity in Action: Malala's commitment to advocating for education for all girls in Pakistan, even in the face of threats and violence from the Taliban, is a testament to her unwavering integrity. She has risked her life to stand up for what she believes is right, refusing to compromise her values for personal safety.

4. The Impact of Authentic Leadership on Organizations

Authentic leadership, with its foundation of integrity, has a profound impact on organizations. It creates a culture of trust, ethical behavior, and accountability, which, in turn, leads to various benefits:

i. Enhanced Employee Engagement: Authentic leaders inspire their team members to engage fully in their work, as they feel valued and supported.

ii. Improved Decision-Making: Ethical decision-making, guided by integrity, leads to better long-term outcomes for organizations.

iii. Increased Loyalty: Team members and stakeholders are more likely to remain loyal to leaders and organizations that prioritize authenticity and integrity.

iv. Stronger Reputation: Authentic leadership enhances an organization's reputation, attracting customers, partners, and top talent.

v. Resilience in Adversity: Organizations led by authentic leaders are better equipped to navigate challenges and crises with their values intact.

5. Cultivating Authentic Leadership

Authentic leadership is not reserved for a select few; it can be cultivated and developed by anyone willing to embark on a journey of self-discovery and personal growth. Here are some steps to cultivate authentic leadership:

i. Self-Reflection: Engage in deep self-reflection to understand your core values, beliefs, and principles. What matters most to you? What do you stand for?

ii. Embrace Vulnerability: Authentic leaders are not afraid to show vulnerability. Being open about your challenges and insecurities can create stronger connections with others.

iii. Act with Integrity: Prioritize integrity in all your actions and decisions. Always choose what is right over what is expedient.

iv. Be Transparent: Practice transparency in your communication, sharing information openly and honestly with your team and stakeholders.

v. Listen Actively: Actively listen to the perspectives and feedback of others. Understand their viewpoints and consider their input in decision-making.

vi. Seek Feedback: Encourage feedback from others about your leadership style and areas for improvement. Use feedback as a tool for growth.

6. Conclusion: The Ethical Compass of Authentic Leadership

Authentic leadership, guided by integrity, serves as the ethical compass that guides leaders in their decision-making journey. It is a powerful force that fosters trust, credibility, and ethical behavior within organizations. As exemplified by leaders like Nelson Mandela, Warren Buffett, and Malala Yousafzai, authenticity and integrity are not mere concepts but powerful forces for positive change in the world. In an era where ethical leadership is more critical than ever, authentic leaders who prioritize integrity in their decision-making have the potential to inspire and transform individuals, organizations, and societies alike.

Chapter 4: Applying the Wisdom of Wolves

Applying Wolf Wisdom: In the dynamic and competitive landscape of modern business, leaders seek inspiration from various sources to navigate challenges and foster success. One such source of inspiration is the wisdom of wolves. Wolf packs, with their complex social structures, effective teamwork, and ability to thrive in diverse environments, offer valuable insights for leaders striving to build cohesive teams, foster a sense of belonging, and embrace diversity within their organizations. In this exploration, we will provide practical insights into how leaders can apply the wisdom of wolves in modern business settings, offering strategies to create high-performing teams and inclusive work environments.

1. The Foundation of Wolf Wisdom

Before delving into practical insights, it is essential to understand the foundational principles of wolf wisdom that leaders can apply to their organizations:

i. Pack Dynamics: Wolf packs are structured around hierarchies and roles. Each member plays a distinct role that contributes to the pack's survival and success.

ii. Communication: Wolves rely on a variety of vocalizations, body language, and scent marking to communicate with one another. Effective communication is crucial for coordinating activities and maintaining social order.

iii. Cooperation: Wolves are highly cooperative animals. They work together to hunt, protect their territory, and raise their young. Cooperation is essential for their survival.

iv. Inclusivity: Wolf packs are diverse in terms of age, gender, and abilities. Each member is valued for their unique contributions to the pack.

v. Resilience: Wolves are resilient creatures, adapting to changing environments and overcoming adversity. Their ability to bounce back from challenges is a key factor in their success.

2. Building Cohesive Teams

Leaders can draw inspiration from wolf pack dynamics to build cohesive teams within their organizations. Here are practical insights for achieving this:

i. Define Roles and Responsibilities: Like wolf packs, teams should have clearly defined roles and responsibilities. Leaders should ensure that each team member understands their role and how it contributes to the team's goals.

ii. Foster Communication: Effective communication is the glue that holds teams together. Encourage open and honest communication among team members. Create opportunities for regular feedback and collaboration.

iii. Develop Trust: Trust is the foundation of cohesive teams. Leaders should model trustworthiness and create an environment where team members trust one another. Trust enables risk-taking and innovation.

iv. Embrace Diversity of Skills: Wolf packs benefit from the diverse skills of their members. In teams, leaders should recognize and value the unique skills and perspectives each team member brings to the table. Encourage cross-functional collaboration.

v. Promote Team Bonding: Wolf packs have strong social bonds. Team bonding activities, both within and outside the workplace, can strengthen connections among team members and foster a sense of unity.

3. Fostering Belonging and Inclusivity

The sense of belonging is crucial for employee engagement and well-being. Leaders can apply lessons from wolf pack inclusivity to create a culture of belonging in their organizations:

i. Value Diversity: Wolf packs include members of different ages and abilities. Organizations should embrace diversity in terms of gender, race, age, and background. Diversity enriches perspectives and drives innovation.

ii. Create an Inclusive Culture: Leaders should actively promote an inclusive culture where all employees feel valued and respected. Encourage open discussions about diversity and inclusion.

iii. Provide Opportunities for Growth: In wolf packs, young wolves learn from their elders. Organizations can adopt mentorship and development programs to facilitate knowledge sharing and skill development among employees.

iv. Celebrate Differences: Just as wolves celebrate the strengths of individual pack members, organizations should celebrate the unique qualities and contributions of their employees. Recognize and reward diverse talents.

v. Encourage Collaboration: Wolf packs rely on cooperation for their survival. Organizations should foster collaboration among employees, breaking down silos and encouraging cross-functional teamwork.

4. Embracing Diversity in Leadership

Diversity in leadership positions is essential for organizations to thrive in today's globalized world. Here are practical insights for leaders looking to embrace diversity in their leadership teams:

i. Diverse Recruitment: Actively seek diverse candidates when filling leadership positions. Implement inclusive hiring practices that attract candidates from different backgrounds.

ii. Inclusive Leadership Development: Provide leadership development opportunities for employees from underrepresented groups. Mentorship programs can help aspiring leaders from diverse backgrounds.

iii. Diverse Perspectives: Embrace diverse perspectives in decision-making. Leaders should actively seek input from team members with varied backgrounds and experiences.

iv. Inclusive Policies: Implement policies that promote diversity and inclusion in the workplace. These policies may include flexible work arrangements, diversity training, and support for employee resource groups.

v. Accountability: Hold leaders accountable for promoting diversity and inclusion within their teams. Set diversity goals and regularly assess progress.

5. Navigating Challenges and Building Resilience

Just as wolf packs navigate challenges in their natural environments, organizations must be prepared to face adversity. Leaders can learn from the resilience of wolves to navigate challenges effectively:

i. Adaptability: Organizations should foster a culture of adaptability, where employees are encouraged to embrace change and respond effectively to unexpected challenges.

ii. Leadership During Crisis: Wolf packs are known for their strong leadership during crises. Leaders should remain calm and provide clear guidance to their teams in times of crisis.

iii. Learning from Failure: Wolves learn from both success and failure. Organizations should encourage a growth mindset, where failure is seen as an opportunity for learning and improvement.

iv. Collaboration in Adversity: In challenging times, wolf packs rely on cooperation. Organizations should emphasize the importance of teamwork and support among employees when facing difficulties.

v. Resilience Training: Provide resilience training and resources for employees to help them cope with stress and adversity effectively.

6. Conclusion: A Blueprint for Thriving in the Modern Business Jungle

The wisdom of wolves offers a compelling blueprint for leaders seeking to build cohesive teams, foster a sense of belonging, and embrace diversity within their organizations. By drawing inspiration from pack dynamics, leaders can create a workplace culture that values trust, communication, cooperation, and resilience.

In today's complex and competitive business landscape, organizations that apply these insights from wolf wisdom are better equipped to thrive, adapt to change, and achieve lasting success. Just as wolf packs navigate the challenges of their natural environments, modern organizations can navigate the challenges of the business jungle with a strong sense of unity, inclusivity, and resilience, guided by the wisdom of these remarkable creatures.

Leadership Development: Leadership development is a continuous journey of self-discovery, growth, and refinement. In the pursuit of effective leadership, individuals and organizations are increasingly turning to nature for inspiration. The wilderness, with its unforgiving challenges and timeless wisdom, provides a powerful backdrop for leadership development programs and initiatives. In this comprehensive discussion, we will explore the concept of wilderness-inspired leadership development, delve into wilderness-based training and team-building exercises, and examine how they enhance leadership skills.

1. The Call of the Wild: Nature's Lessons for Leadership

Nature has been a source of inspiration for leaders throughout history. From the strategies of military leaders like Sun Tzu, who drew insights from the natural world in "The Art of War," to the leadership principles embodied by animals like wolves, bees, and dolphins, nature offers profound lessons in leadership. These lessons include adaptability, resilience, teamwork, and balance.

i. Adaptability: Nature is the ultimate teacher of adaptability. It demonstrates how living organisms evolve and adjust to changing environments, much like effective leaders who must adapt to shifting circumstances.

ii. Resilience: Natural ecosystems endure countless challenges and yet continue to thrive. Leaders can learn from nature's resilience in the face of adversity and apply this to their own leadership journeys.

iii. Teamwork: Collaborative behaviors are evident throughout the natural world, from the intricate communication of ants to the coordinated hunting of wolf packs. Nature emphasizes the importance of teamwork and shared goals.

iv. Balance: Ecosystems maintain a delicate balance between various species and environmental factors. Leaders can draw insights from this equilibrium to navigate the complexities of organizational dynamics.

2. The Rise of Wilderness-Inspired Leadership Development

Wilderness-inspired leadership development is a contemporary approach that leverages the transformative power of nature to nurture leadership skills. It often involves experiential learning, where participants are taken out of their comfort zones and into the wilderness to confront challenges that require leadership qualities such as decision-making, communication, adaptability, and resilience.

i. Experiential Learning: Wilderness programs immerse participants in scenarios that demand real-time problem-solving and decision-making. These immersive experiences help individuals translate theory into practice.

ii. Environmental Consciousness: Interactions with nature foster a greater sense of environmental responsibility and sustainability, which are increasingly important leadership qualities in an environmentally conscious world.

iii. Personal Growth: Wilderness experiences challenge individuals to discover their strengths, weaknesses, and leadership styles. The process of self-discovery can be profound, leading to personal growth and increased self-awareness.

3. Key Components of Wilderness-Inspired Leadership Development

Wilderness-inspired leadership development programs encompass a range of activities and approaches that harness the power of nature to enhance leadership skills. Some key components include:

i. Outdoor Expeditions: Participants embark on outdoor expeditions that require teamwork, navigation, and problem-solving. These expeditions can include hiking, camping, rafting, and more.

ii. Survival Skills: Learning survival skills, such as fire-building, shelter construction, and wilderness first aid, not only enhances practical knowledge but also fosters resilience and adaptability.

iii. Leadership Challenges: Participants face leadership challenges in the wilderness, such as leading a group through rugged terrain or making critical decisions in high-stress situations.

iv. Reflection and Debriefing: After wilderness experiences, reflection and debriefing sessions provide an opportunity for participants to analyze their actions, decisions, and leadership behaviors.

v. Nature Immersion: Time spent in nature, away from digital distractions, allows participants to reconnect with the natural world and experience its calming and inspirational effects.

4. The Impact on Leadership Skills

Wilderness-inspired leadership development has a profound impact on leadership skills. Participants often report growth in the following areas:

i. Decision-Making: Wilderness experiences force individuals to make decisions quickly and decisively, enhancing their decision-making skills.

ii. Communication: Effective communication is essential in the wilderness to coordinate actions and ensure safety. Participants develop clearer and more concise communication skills.

iii. Problem-Solving: Wilderness challenges require creative problem-solving, encouraging individuals to think outside the box and explore innovative solutions.

iv. Resilience: Confronting adversity in the wilderness fosters resilience and the ability to bounce back from setbacks.

v. Adaptability: Navigating unpredictable natural environments teaches adaptability, a critical skill in today's rapidly changing business landscape.

vi. Self-Awareness: Wilderness experiences often lead to greater self-awareness as participants confront their fears, limitations, and leadership styles.

5. Case Studies: Wilderness-Inspired Leadership Programs

To understand the practical application of wilderness-inspired leadership development, let's explore two case studies.

i. Outward Bound

Outward Bound is a renowned organization that offers wilderness-based leadership development programs. Participants engage in activities such as rock climbing, canoeing, and backpacking, where they must work together to overcome challenges. Outward Bound emphasizes experiential learning, personal growth, and leadership development.

ii. National Outdoor Leadership School (NOLS)

NOLS is dedicated to teaching outdoor skills and leadership in the wilderness. Participants learn practical skills like navigation, wilderness medicine, and Leave No Trace principles. The immersive nature of NOLS programs allows participants to develop leadership skills in a real-world context.

6. Challenges and Considerations

While wilderness-inspired leadership development offers numerous benefits, there are challenges and considerations to keep in mind:

i. Safety: Safety in the wilderness is paramount. Programs must have robust safety protocols and qualified instructors.

ii. Accessibility: Not everyone has access to wilderness areas, which can limit participation.

iii. Cost: Wilderness programs can be costly, potentially excluding individuals or organizations with limited budgets.

iv. Environmental Impact: Programs should prioritize environmental sustainability and minimize their impact on natural ecosystems.

7. Conclusion: Leading with Nature's Guidance

Wilderness-inspired leadership development is a powerful tool for individuals and organizations seeking to enhance leadership skills, foster personal growth, and embrace the wisdom of nature. By immersing participants in challenging outdoor environments, these programs provide unique opportunities for experiential learning and self-discovery. As leaders navigate the complexities of the modern business landscape, they can draw inspiration from the adaptability, resilience, and teamwork observed in the natural world. In doing so, they can lead with a deeper understanding of themselves, their teams, and the environment, ultimately becoming more effective and impactful leaders.

Sustainability and Stewardship: Sustainability is the practice of meeting the needs of the present without compromising the ability of future generations to meet their own needs. In the context of leadership, sustainability extends beyond environmental concerns to encompass economic, social, and ethical dimensions. It calls for leaders to make decisions that balance short-term objectives with the long-term well-being of their organizations, society, and the planet.

Stewardship, on the other hand, refers to the responsible management and care of resources, whether they are natural, financial, or human. Leaders who embrace stewardship recognize their duty to safeguard and enhance these resources for the benefit of current and future generations.

2. The Role of Responsible Leadership

Responsible leadership is an approach that aligns with the principles of sustainability and stewardship. It entails a commitment to ethical conduct, transparency, and accountability in decision-making. Responsible leaders take into account not only the immediate consequences of their actions but also the broader and often interconnected effects on various stakeholders and the environment.

i. Ethical Conduct: Responsible leaders uphold high ethical standards in all their actions and decisions. They prioritize fairness, honesty, and integrity.

ii. Transparency: Transparency is crucial for responsible leadership. Leaders should be open and honest about their intentions, actions, and the impact of their decisions.

iii. Accountability: Responsible leaders take responsibility for the outcomes of their decisions, whether positive or negative. They acknowledge mistakes and take corrective action.

iv. Stakeholder Engagement: Leaders consider the perspectives and interests of all stakeholders, including employees, customers, communities, and the environment, when making decisions.

v. Long-Term Perspective: Responsible leaders adopt a long-term perspective, understanding that sustainable success requires planning and action beyond the immediate future.

3. The Three Pillars of Sustainability

Sustainability is often described in terms of three interconnected pillars: **economic**, **social**, and **environmental**. These pillars provide a framework for leaders to assess the impact of their decisions comprehensively.

i. Economic Sustainability: Economic sustainability focuses on the financial viability and profitability of organizations. It emphasizes responsible financial management, investment in innovation, and the creation of long-term economic value.

ii. Social Sustainability: Social sustainability addresses the well-being of employees, customers, and communities. Responsible leaders prioritize issues such as diversity and inclusion, fair labor practices, and community engagement.

iii. Environmental Sustainability: Environmental sustainability revolves around minimizing the negative impact of organizational activities on the environment and promoting practices that support ecological balance. It includes efforts to reduce waste, conserve resources, and mitigate climate change.

4. Strategies for Integrating Sustainability and Stewardship into Leadership

To effectively integrate sustainability and stewardship into leadership practices, leaders can adopt several strategies:

i. Set Clear Sustainability Goals: Leaders should establish clear and measurable sustainability goals for their organizations. These goals can cover areas such as energy efficiency, waste reduction, and social responsibility.

ii. Foster a Culture of Sustainability: Leaders can promote a culture of sustainability by encouraging employees to actively participate in sustainability initiatives and by recognizing and rewarding environmentally responsible behaviors.

iii. Collaborate with Stakeholders: Engaging with stakeholders, including customers, suppliers, and advocacy groups, can provide valuable insights and support for sustainability efforts. Collaboration fosters shared responsibility.

iv. Conduct Sustainability Assessments: Leaders can conduct regular assessments to evaluate the environmental and social impact of their operations. This helps identify areas for improvement and measure progress.

v. Invest in Sustainable Practices: Sustainable practices may require initial investments, but they often yield long-term benefits. Leaders should be willing to invest in technologies and practices that reduce their organization's environmental footprint.

vi. Communicate Sustainability Efforts: Transparent communication about sustainability initiatives builds trust with stakeholders and demonstrates a commitment to responsible leadership.

5. Case Studies in Sustainable Leadership

Let's examine two case studies that exemplify sustainable leadership in action.

i. Patagonia: A Commitment to Environmental Stewardship

Outdoor clothing and gear company Patagonia has become a symbol of sustainable and responsible leadership. Patagonia's founder, Yvon Chouinard, has consistently prioritized environmental stewardship and social responsibility.

Sustainable Practices: Patagonia has adopted a range of sustainable practices, including using recycled materials in its products, implementing fair labor practices in its supply chain, and donating a significant portion of its profits to environmental causes.

Transparency: The company is transparent about its supply chain and environmental impact, providing customers with information to make informed choices.

Activism: Patagonia takes an active role in advocating for environmental conservation and social justice, using its platform to raise awareness and drive positive change.

ii. Unilever: Sustainable Living Plan

Consumer goods giant Unilever has embraced sustainability as a core component of its business strategy through its Sustainable Living Plan.

Environmental Targets: Unilever set ambitious environmental targets, including reducing its carbon footprint and water usage while increasing the sustainability of its agricultural supply chain.

Social Initiatives: The company has launched numerous social initiatives, such as promoting gender equality and improving hygiene and sanitation in developing countries.

Long-Term Commitment: Unilever's commitment to sustainability is not a short-term endeavor; it is integrated into its long-term business strategy.

6. The Intersection of Sustainability, Stewardship, and Profitability

One of the common misconceptions about sustainability and stewardship is that they come at the expense of profitability. However, evidence suggests that responsible leadership can be a driver of long-term financial success.

Cost Savings: Sustainable practices often result in cost savings through reduced resource consumption, improved efficiency, and minimized waste.

Reputation and Brand Value: Organizations that prioritize sustainability and responsible leadership often enjoy enhanced brand reputation and customer loyalty, leading to increased sales and market share.

Risk Mitigation: Sustainability efforts can reduce risks associated with environmental and social issues, such as regulatory fines, supply chain disruptions, and reputational damage.

Innovation: Focusing on sustainability can drive innovation, leading to the development of new products, services, and business models that capture market opportunities.

Investor Interest: Many investors are increasingly considering environmental, social, and governance (ESG) factors when making investment decisions. Companies with strong ESG performance are more likely to attract investment.

7. The Road Ahead: Embracing Responsible Leadership

As the world grapples with pressing challenges, including climate change, social inequality, and resource scarcity, responsible leadership that incorporates sustainability and stewardship is not just a choice; it is an imperative. Leaders who embrace these principles recognize that their decisions have far-reaching consequences on the well-being of their organizations, their stakeholders, and the planet.

By adopting a responsible leadership mindset, leaders can contribute to a more sustainable and equitable future while simultaneously driving long-term organizational success. Sustainability and stewardship are not merely ethical ideals; they are the foundation upon which resilient, adaptable, and thriving organizations are built

Conclusion and Recap:

In the dynamic and challenging landscape of the corporate world, the quest for effective leadership has never been more crucial. The principles of leadership, guided by the wisdom of wolves, offer a compelling source of inspiration and guidance for modern leaders. Throughout this exploration, we've delved deep into the intersection of leadership and the wisdom of wolves, examining how these principles can transform leadership practices in the corporate realm. In this summary, we will highlight the key takeaways from our extensive exploration, emphasizing the transformative potential of integrating these leadership principles into business practices to pave the way for success.

1. Leadership Defined: A Multifaceted Art

Our journey into leadership began with a clear definition that highlighted its evolving nature. Leadership is not a one-size-fits-all concept; it encompasses a diverse range of skills and attributes. These include vision, decisiveness, adaptability, courage, resilience, empathy, authenticity, and effective communication. Effective leadership in the corporate world demands a dynamic blend of these qualities.

2. The Wisdom of Wolves: Nature's Leadership Lessons

The wisdom of wolves, drawn from their intricate pack dynamics, provided a rich source of leadership insights. Wolves are renowned for their teamwork, communication, hierarchy, adaptability, and resilience. These lessons from the wild underscored the importance of cooperation, clear communication, effective teamwork, and adaptability in corporate leadership.

3. Exceptional Leadership Qualities

Delving into the essential qualities of exceptional leaders, we highlighted the significance of vision, decisiveness, adaptability, courage, and empathy. Visionary leaders set a clear direction for their organizations, motivating and inspiring their teams. Decisiveness is crucial for making timely choices in the face of uncertainty. Adaptability ensures leaders can navigate change and seize opportunities. Courage empowers leaders to make difficult decisions and stand up for what's right. Finally, empathy fosters strong interpersonal connections and understanding within teams.

4. Resilience and Perseverance: Pillars of Leadership

Our exploration emphasized the critical importance of resilience and perseverance in leadership. Exceptional leaders often face adversity and setbacks on their journey. Resilience enables them to bounce back from challenges, maintaining their commitment to their vision. Perseverance is the determination to persist in the face of obstacles, ensuring leaders stay the course even when the path is difficult.

5. The Power of Empathy and Emotional Intelligence

Empathy and emotional intelligence emerged as pivotal elements of effective leadership. Leaders who understand and connect with their team members on an emotional level can build trust, inspire motivation, and foster a positive work environment. The social bonds of wolf packs highlighted how strong interpersonal connections are fundamental to leadership success.

6. Leading by Example: A Compelling Leadership Approach

Leading by example is a potent approach to leadership, inspiring and motivating teams through the actions of the leader. Through compelling anecdotes and case studies, we explored how leaders who embody the values and behaviors they expect from their teams can create a culture of excellence and integrity.

7. The Art of Effective Communication

Effective communication is a cornerstone of leadership. We investigated various communication techniques, both verbal and non-verbal, that leaders can employ to promote collaboration and trust within their teams. Clear and empathetic communication fosters an open and supportive work environment.

8. Authentic Leadership: The Crucial Role of Integrity

Authentic leadership, grounded in integrity, emerged as a paramount concept. Leaders who are true to their values and consistently demonstrate honesty and ethical decision-making inspire trust and credibility. Integrity is the ethical compass that guides leaders through complex choices.

9. Integrating Sustainability and Stewardship

Leadership today transcends organizational boundaries to consider the broader impact on society and the environment. Responsible leadership incorporates sustainability and stewardship principles, ensuring that decisions prioritize long-term well-being over short-term gains. By adopting this mindset, leaders can create a sustainable future for their organizations and the planet.

10. Embracing the Wisdom of Wolves in Corporate Leadership

As we conclude our journey through the wisdom of wolves and its application in corporate leadership, let's summarize the key takeaways:

i. Leadership is Multifaceted: Leadership encompasses a diverse range of qualities and skills, requiring adaptability and versatility.

ii. Nature's Leadership Lessons: The wisdom of wolves teaches us the importance of teamwork, communication, adaptability, and resilience in leadership.

iii. **Exceptional Leadership Qualities**: Exceptional leaders possess vision, decisiveness, adaptability, courage, and empathy.

iv. **Resilience and Perseverance**: Leaders must cultivate resilience to bounce back from challenges and perseverance to stay committed to their goals.

v. **Empathy and Emotional Intelligence**: Understanding and connecting with team members on an emotional level are crucial for effective leadership.

vi. **Leading by Example**: Leaders who lead by example inspire and motivate their teams through their actions.

vii. **Effective Communication**: Clear and empathetic communication is essential for building trust and collaboration.

viii. **Authentic Leadership**: Authentic leaders prioritize integrity and ethical decision-making, earning trust and credibility.

ix. **Sustainability and Stewardship**: Responsible leadership integrates sustainability and stewardship principles to consider the long-term impact on society and the environment.

x. **Transformative Potential**: Integrating the wisdom of wolves into corporate leadership practices can transform organizations, fostering a culture of excellence, integrity, and sustainability.

In today's fast-paced and complex business environment, leaders who draw inspiration from nature's wisdom and embody these principles have the potential to navigate challenges effectively, inspire their teams, and drive their organizations toward lasting success. By embracing the multifaceted nature of leadership, nurturing essential qualities, and weaving sustainability and stewardship into their leadership fabric, leaders can pave the way to lasting success.

Chapter 5: Leading a Sales Team:

Sales teams are the lifeblood of many organizations. They are responsible for revenue generation, client acquisition, and often the public face of the company. Effectively leading and motivating sales teams is a critical aspect of ensuring business success. In this comprehensive exploration, we will delve into the strategies that leaders can employ to lead and motivate sales teams, with a particular focus on coaching for excellence.

1. The Role of Sales Leadership

Effective sales leadership is essential for guiding teams toward their goals, whether that involves meeting revenue targets, acquiring new clients, or fostering client relationships. Sales leaders play a pivotal role in setting the tone, providing direction, and cultivating a positive and high-performing sales culture.

i. Vision Setting: Sales leaders must articulate a clear and inspiring vision that aligns with the organization's objectives. A compelling vision serves as a guiding star for the team.

ii. Goal Alignment: Sales leaders align individual and team goals with broader organizational objectives, ensuring that everyone is working toward a common purpose.

iii. Strategy Development: Crafting effective sales strategies and tactics is a key responsibility of sales leaders. This includes defining target markets, sales channels, and pricing strategies.

iv. Motivation: Sales leaders inspire and motivate their teams to push beyond their comfort zones, emphasizing the importance of resilience and perseverance in the face of rejection and setbacks.

v. Coaching and Development: Effective sales leadership involves coaching team members to enhance their skills and reach their full potential. This is where coaching for excellence becomes particularly crucial.

2. The Power of Coaching for Excellence

Coaching for excellence is a proactive approach to developing sales team members' skills and capabilities to achieve peak performance. It involves providing guidance, feedback, and support to help individuals reach their highest potential. This coaching methodology is grounded in the belief that excellence is a journey, not a destination.

i. Individualized Approach: Effective coaching recognizes that each sales team member is unique. Coaches tailor their guidance to address individual strengths, weaknesses, and development areas.

ii. Constructive Feedback: Coaches provide specific, constructive, and actionable feedback to help salespeople understand their performance and make improvements.

iii. Skill Enhancement: Coaching for excellence focuses on enhancing crucial sales skills, including prospecting, communication, negotiation, objection handling, and closing deals.

iv. Goal Setting: Coaches assist sales team members in setting challenging yet achievable goals, helping them stay motivated and focused on their objectives.

v. Accountability: Coaches hold salespeople accountable for their commitments and actions, fostering a sense of responsibility and ownership.

3. Strategies for Leading and Motivating Sales Teams

Let's explore strategies that leaders can employ to effectively lead and motivate their sales teams.

i. Lead by Example: Leading by example is a powerful motivational tool. When sales leaders demonstrate dedication, professionalism, and a strong work ethic, they inspire their teams to do the same.

ii. Clear Communication: Transparent and open communication is essential. Sales teams should have a clear understanding of their roles, expectations, and the company's vision.

iii. Recognition and Rewards: Acknowledging and rewarding achievements, both big and small, boosts motivation. Recognize top performers through incentives, bonuses, or public recognition.

iv. Ongoing Training: Continuous training and development opportunities keep sales teams engaged and competitive. Training should cover product knowledge, sales techniques, and soft skills.

v. Sales Metrics and Data: Use data-driven insights to set performance benchmarks and track progress. Regularly review sales metrics and provide feedback to guide improvements.

vi. Incentive Programs: Design incentive programs that align with sales targets. These can include commission structures, bonuses, or contests to boost motivation.

vii. Team Building: Foster a sense of camaraderie and collaboration within the team. Team-building activities and outings can improve morale and build stronger bonds.

viii. Flexibility: Empower sales team members by allowing flexibility in their work arrangements. This can enhance work-life balance and job satisfaction.

ix. Constructive Feedback: Provide timely and constructive feedback that helps salespeople understand areas for improvement and how to address them.

x. Career Pathways: Offer clear career development pathways within the organization. When salespeople see opportunities for growth and advancement, they are more likely to stay motivated.

4. Coaching for Excellence: A Holistic Approach

Coaching for excellence is a multifaceted process that requires a holistic approach to nurturing sales team members' potential.

i. Building Trust: Effective coaching starts with building trust. Salespeople should feel safe and supported in discussing their challenges and aspirations.

ii. Active Listening: Coaches must be active listeners, paying close attention to sales team members' concerns, questions, and ideas.

iii. Goal Alignment: Align coaching efforts with individual and team goals. Ensure that coaching sessions are focused on helping salespeople achieve these objectives.

iv. Constructive Feedback: Feedback should be delivered constructively, focusing on behaviors and outcomes rather than personal traits.

v. Skill Enhancement: Identify key sales skills that need improvement and work collaboratively to enhance them. Role-playing and scenario-based training can be effective tools.

vi. Mentorship: Mentorship programs can complement coaching efforts, pairing less experienced salespeople with seasoned veterans who can provide guidance and insights.

vii. Evaluation and Adjustment: Continuously assess the impact of coaching efforts and adjust strategies based on results. A dynamic approach ensures ongoing improvement.

5. Case Studies in Leading and Motivating Sales Teams

Two case studies illustrate the effective application of strategies for leading and motivating sales teams and coaching for excellence.

i. Salesforce: A Culture of Continuous Learning

Salesforce, a global leader in customer relationship management (CRM) software, places a strong emphasis on continuous learning and development for its sales teams. The company offers extensive training resources, certification programs, and regular coaching sessions. Salesforce's commitment to coaching and skill enhancement contributes to its ongoing success and rapid growth.

ii. HubSpot: Incentives and Recognition

HubSpot, a marketing and sales software provider, has implemented innovative incentive programs and recognition initiatives to motivate its sales teams. The company offers a culture of recognition, where top performers receive awards, public acknowledgment, and even a prestigious Club Award. HubSpot's incentive programs and recognition culture have contributed to high levels of motivation and employee retention.

6. The Transformative Impact of Effective Leadership and Coaching

Effective leadership and coaching for excellence have the potential to transform sales teams and drive business success in various ways:

i. Improved Performance: Sales teams that receive effective leadership and coaching consistently outperform their peers, leading to increased revenue and growth.

ii. Motivated Workforce: Motivated salespeople are more engaged and productive, contributing to a positive work environment and reducing turnover.

iii. Enhanced Skills: Coaching for excellence sharpens sales skills, improving communication, negotiation, and objection handling, leading to higher closing rates.

iv. Greater Resilience: Sales teams that receive coaching are better equipped to bounce back from rejections and setbacks

Part II: Sales
Chapter 6: The Art of Sales

Sales, often referred to as the lifeblood of any business, is a dynamic and multifaceted field that encompasses a wide range of industries, strategies, and techniques. To delve into the world of sales is to explore the art of persuasion, negotiation, and relationship-building that drives business growth. In this comprehensive exploration, we will dissect the various types of sales, the key dynamics that shape the sales landscape, and the vital role that sales plays as a cornerstone of business success.

1. Types of Sales

Sales can be categorized into several distinct types, each with its unique characteristics, target audience, and strategies. Understanding these types is crucial for tailoring sales efforts to specific market segments.

i. Business-to-Consumer (B2C) Sales: B2C sales involve selling products or services directly to individual consumers. These sales often occur through retail outlets, e-commerce platforms, or direct sales representatives. B2C sales emphasize marketing strategies that appeal to individual needs and preferences.

ii. Business-to-Business (B2B) Sales: B2B sales involve selling products or services to other businesses. These transactions tend to be more complex and involve longer sales cycles. B2B sales require a deep understanding of the needs and challenges of the client's business.

iii. Inside Sales: Inside sales teams operate remotely, using phone calls, emails, and virtual meetings to engage with prospects and customers. This type of sales is cost-effective and efficient for reaching a broad audience.

iv. Field Sales: Field sales involve sales representatives who travel to meet with clients and prospects face-to-face. This approach allows for a more personalized and relationship-focused sales process.

v. Retail Sales: Retail sales occur in physical stores, where products or services are sold directly to consumers. Retail sales require effective visual merchandising and customer service.

vi. Online Sales (E-commerce): E-commerce sales take place on digital platforms, such as websites or mobile apps. The online sales landscape is highly competitive and demands a strong online presence, user-friendly interfaces, and efficient logistics.

vii. Direct Sales: Direct sales involve sales representatives who promote and sell products or services directly to consumers in their homes or workplaces. This method often relies on personal relationships and persuasive skills.

viii. Consultative Sales: Consultative sales involve a deeper level of engagement, with salespeople acting as consultants who understand the client's needs and offer tailored solutions. This approach builds trust and fosters long-term relationships.

2. Dynamics of the Sales Landscape

The dynamics of the sales landscape are continually evolving, influenced by factors such as technology, market trends, and consumer behavior. To succeed in sales, professionals must adapt to these dynamics and leverage them to their advantage.

i. Technology Disruption: Advancements in technology have transformed the sales process. From customer relationship management (CRM) software to artificial intelligence (AI) tools for sales forecasting, technology plays a pivotal role in optimizing sales operations.

ii. Data-Driven Decision-Making: Sales teams now have access to vast amounts of data that can inform decision-making. Data analytics and customer insights help sales professionals target the right audience and tailor their approach.

iii. Omnichannel Sales: Consumers expect a seamless experience across various channels, including online, mobile, and physical stores.

Successful sales strategies incorporate omnichannel approaches that connect with customers where they are.

iv. **Customer-Centricity**: Customer expectations have shifted toward personalized experiences. Sales professionals must prioritize understanding the customer's journey, needs, and preferences.

v. **Sales Enablement**: Sales enablement tools and processes empower sales teams with the resources, content, and training they need to sell effectively. This includes providing product information, sales collateral, and training modules.

vi. **Social Selling**: Social media platforms have become powerful tools for sales professionals to connect with prospects, share content, and build relationships. Social selling emphasizes engagement and authenticity.

vii. **Sales Automation**: Automation tools, such as email marketing automation and chatbots, streamline routine tasks, allowing sales teams to focus on higher-value activities, like relationship-building.

viii. **Globalization**: The globalization of markets has expanded the reach of sales efforts. Companies are increasingly engaging in international sales, requiring a deep understanding of global cultures and regulations.

ix. **Sales Ethics and Compliance**: Ethical considerations and regulatory compliance have gained prominence in the sales landscape. Sales professionals must adhere to ethical standards and navigate complex compliance requirements.

3. Sales as a Vital Component of Business

Sales is undeniably a vital component of business success. It serves as the engine that drives revenue, profitability, and growth. Without effective sales strategies and execution, even the most innovative products or services may go unnoticed or underutilized.

i. **Revenue Generation**: Sales teams are responsible for converting leads and prospects into paying customers. Revenue generation is the lifeblood of any business, funding operations, innovation, and expansion.

ii. Market Expansion: Effective sales efforts enable businesses to expand into new markets, both domestically and internationally. Sales teams identify growth opportunities and develop market entry strategies.

iii. Customer Acquisition and Retention: Sales professionals not only acquire new customers but also play a crucial role in retaining and nurturing existing ones. Customer retention is often more cost-effective than customer acquisition.

iv. Competitive Advantage: A strong sales function provides a competitive advantage by effectively positioning products or services in the market, differentiating them from competitors, and securing market share.

v. Product Feedback: Sales teams serve as a valuable source of feedback from the field. They gather insights on customer needs, preferences, and pain points, which can inform product development and innovation.

vi. Profitability: Profitability is closely tied to sales performance. Effective pricing strategies, upselling, and cross-selling contribute to higher profit margins.

vii. Brand Reputation: The way sales teams interact with customers influences brand reputation. Positive customer experiences and relationships bolster brand trust and loyalty.

viii. Economic Impact: Sales activities have a significant economic impact, driving economic growth, job creation, and innovation within communities and regions.

4. Challenges and Strategies in Sales Leadership

Leading and managing sales teams presents unique challenges that require specific strategies:

i. Sales Team Motivation: Maintaining sales team motivation is an ongoing challenge. Leaders must offer incentives, recognition, and career growth opportunities to keep teams engaged and productive.

ii. Sales Training and Development: Continuous training and development are essential to equip sales teams with the latest skills and knowledge. Investing in sales education ensures teams stay competitive.

iii. Sales Forecasting: Accurate sales forecasting is critical for resource allocation and business planning. Leaders should leverage data analytics and sales intelligence tools for precise forecasts.

iv. Sales Performance Metrics: Identifying the right Key Performance Indicators (KPIs) and measuring sales performance against these metrics is essential for tracking progress and making data-driven decisions.

v. Sales Strategy Alignment: Sales strategies must align with broader organizational goals and market dynamics. Effective communication and collaboration between sales leaders and other departments are vital.

vi. Change Management: Adapting to evolving market dynamics and technology requires effective change management strategies to ensure that sales teams can embrace and thrive in new environments.

vii. Sales Ethics: Upholding ethical standards is paramount in sales leadership. Leaders should establish clear ethical guidelines and promote a culture of integrity within their teams.

viii. Crisis Management: Sales leaders must be prepared to navigate crises, such as economic downturns or unforeseen disruptions. Resilience and adaptability are key traits in such situations.

5. Case Studies in Sales Excellence

Two case studies illustrate the significance of effective sales strategies and their impact on business success:

i. Apple Inc.: The Power of Branding and Innovation

Apple is renowned for its exceptional sales strategies, underpinned by innovative products and strong branding. The company's product launches generate significant buzz and anticipation, driving customer demand. Apple's retail stores provide a unique customer experience that fosters brand loyalty and sales.

ii. Amazon.com: Customer-Centric Sales Approach

Amazon's success is attributed in part to its customer-centric sales approach. The company prioritizes customer satisfaction, offering a wide range of products, competitive pricing, and convenient delivery options. Amazon's sales platform is designed for ease of use and personalization, creating a seamless shopping experience.

6. The Future of Sales

The future of sales promises continued evolution, driven by technology, changing consumer behavior, and global dynamics. To thrive in this future landscape, businesses and sales professionals must remain agile, customer-focused, and adaptable.

i. AI and Automation: Artificial intelligence and automation will play an increasingly prominent role in sales, from chatbots providing customer support to AI-driven sales forecasting and predictive analytics.

ii. Personalization: Customers expect highly personalized experiences. Sales teams will need to leverage data and technology to tailor their offerings and interactions.

iii. Sustainability: Ethical and sustainable practices will gain more importance in sales. Businesses that prioritize sustainability will resonate with environmentally conscious consumers.

iv. Remote Sales: Remote sales and virtual selling will continue to grow, requiring sales teams to master virtual communication and relationship-building.

v. Hybrid Sales Models: Hybrid sales models, combining online and offline channels, will become more prevalent as businesses seek to meet customers where they are.

vi. Cybersecurity: Sales professionals will need to be well-versed in cybersecurity to protect customer data and ensure trust in online transactions.

vii. Globalization: Expanding into international markets will remain a growth strategy for many businesses, necessitating cross-cultural competence in sales teams.

viii. Industry-Specific Sales: Sales professionals in specialized industries, such as healthcare or technology, will require industry-specific knowledge and compliance expertise.

7. Conclusion: Sales as the Engine of Business Growth

In conclusion, the world of sales is a dynamic and multifaceted arena that drives business success. Understanding the types of sales, the dynamics shaping the sales landscape, and the vital role of sales as a cornerstone of business is essential for organizations and sales professionals alike. The future of sales promises exciting opportunities, challenges, and innovations as technology and consumer preferences continue to evolve. Effective sales leadership, supported by adaptability and a customer-centric approach, will remain fundamental to achieving growth and profitability in the ever-changing business landscape.

Chapter 7: Sales Skills

Sales is both an art and a science. To excel in this field, professionals must master a range of skills that encompass building relationships, negotiation, and persuasion. In this chapter, we will delve deep into these critical aspects of sales mastery and draw inspiration from case studies of successful salespeople who have achieved remarkable results through their expertise in these areas.

Building Relationships: The Foundation of Sales Mastery

1.1 The Power of Relationships in Sales

In the world of sales, relationships are the bedrock upon which successful transactions are built. While product quality, pricing, and marketing strategies certainly play vital roles, it is the power of relationships that often tips the scales in favor of a sale. Whether you're selling a complex B2B service or a consumer product, nurturing and leveraging relationships can significantly impact your sales success.

Trust and Credibility: At the heart of every successful sale is trust. Building trust takes time, effort, and consistent communication. When customers trust you, they are more likely to believe in the value of your product or service. A strong relationship with a client can make them more willing to take a leap of faith, especially when making a substantial purchase. Your credibility, gained through past successful interactions, can ease any concerns they may have.

Customer Retention: Acquiring new customers can be costly and time-consuming. Maintaining relationships with existing customers, on the other hand, is often more efficient and cost-effective. When customers feel valued and respected, they are more likely to remain loyal. This loyalty can translate into repeat business and referrals, both of which are invaluable in sustaining a thriving sales operation.

Personalization: Understanding your customers on a personal level is a key advantage of relationship-based sales. When you know your clients' preferences, needs, and pain points, you can tailor your sales approach to speak directly to them. Personalization not only increases the likelihood of a sale but also enhances the overall customer experience, which can lead to positive word-of-mouth recommendations.

Emotional Connection: People are more likely to make buying decisions based on emotions rather than logic. Strong relationships tap into this human tendency by fostering emotional connections with customers. Salespeople who genuinely care about their clients and their success can elicit positive emotions, making the buying decision feel more natural and less forced.

Handling Objections: In sales, objections are par for the course. A strong relationship can make handling objections easier. When a customer raises concerns or objections, they are more likely to communicate openly with a salesperson they trust. This transparency allows for a more constructive discussion, where objections can be addressed and resolved effectively.

Feedback and Improvement: Maintaining relationships doesn't just benefit the salesperson; it also benefits the product or service being sold. Through ongoing interactions with customers, salespeople can gather valuable feedback and insights. This feedback can inform product improvements, leading to better customer satisfaction and increased sales in the long run.

Long-Term Partnerships: Successful salespeople view each transaction as the beginning of a long-term relationship, not the end. Building strong relationships can lead to partnerships that span years, if not decades. These long-term partnerships often yield a continuous stream of business, as clients return for additional products or services and refer others.

Competitive Advantage: In today's competitive business landscape, differentiation is crucial. Building strong relationships can be a significant differentiator. Customers often choose to do business with companies they feel a connection to, even if competitors offer similar products or services. A solid relationship can set your business apart from the competition.

In conclusion, the power of relationships in sales cannot be overstated. Trust, credibility, customer retention, personalization, emotional connection, objection handling, feedback, long-term partnerships, and competitive advantage are just a few of the benefits that result from investing in strong relationships with your clients. To succeed in sales, remember that you're not just selling a product or service; you're building relationships that can transform one-time buyers into loyal, lifelong customers.

1.2 Case Study: Jill Rowley - The Social Selling Maven

Case Study: Jill Rowley - The Social Selling Maven

Background: Jill Rowley is widely recognized as a pioneer in the realm of social selling. Her journey from a successful corporate career to becoming a social selling evangelist serves as an exemplary case of building strong customer relationships through authentic engagement and modern sales techniques.

Challenges: Jill faced the challenge of adapting to the rapidly changing landscape of sales. She realized that traditional methods were becoming less effective and that customers were increasingly making buying decisions based on digital interactions. She needed to find a way to leverage social media platforms to build meaningful relationships with her prospects and clients.

Strategy: Jill Rowley embraced social selling as a core part of her sales strategy. She recognized the importance of authenticity and genuine engagement in building lasting relationships. Her approach involved:

Education: Jill invested in learning about various social media platforms and how to use them effectively for sales purposes. She became an expert in leveraging LinkedIn, Twitter, and other platforms to connect with her audience.

Content Creation: She consistently produced valuable content that addressed her target audience's pain points and needs. This content positioned her as a thought leader and provided a reason for prospects to engage with her.

Personalization: Jill made an effort to personalize her outreach. Instead of sending generic sales pitches, she focused on building connections by commenting on prospects' posts, sharing relevant content, and sending personalized messages.

Listening and Engagement: She actively listened to her audience, paying attention to their interests and concerns. This allowed her to engage in meaningful conversations and provide tailored solutions.

Results: Jill Rowley's dedication to social selling and relationship-building bore remarkable fruit:

Increased Reach: Her social media presence expanded significantly, connecting her with a broader audience of potential clients.

Enhanced Credibility: By consistently sharing valuable insights and engaging authentically, she established herself as a trusted authority in her field.

High Conversion Rates: Her approach led to higher conversion rates compared to traditional cold outreach methods. Prospects were more receptive to her messages because they felt a genuine connection.

Loyal Client Base: Jill's clients became long-term partners, repeatedly seeking her expertise and referring her to others.

Conclusion: Jill Rowley's journey from a traditional sales background to becoming a social selling maven underscores the transformative power of building customer relationships through authentic engagement and modern sales techniques. Her case serves as an inspiration for sales professionals seeking to thrive in an ever-evolving sales landscape where relationships are at the heart of success. By focusing on education, content, personalization, and genuine engagement, Jill Rowley has proven that social selling is not just a trend but a powerful strategy for building and sustaining customer relationships.

2.1 The Significance of Negotiation in Sales

Negotiation is the cornerstone of successful sales. It is the art of reaching mutually beneficial agreements between a seller and a buyer, and its significance cannot be overstated. Effective negotiation skills are essential for closing deals, building strong customer relationships, and maximizing profitability. Here's a closer look at the significance of negotiations in sales:

Closing Deals: Negotiations are often the final step in the sales process, where the terms and conditions of the sale are hammered out. A skilled negotiator can bridge the gap between what the buyer wants and what the seller can provide. Without effective negotiation, deals may stall or fall through entirely.

Maximizing Value: Negotiations allow both parties to extract the maximum value from a transaction. Sellers aim to secure the highest price and most favorable terms, while buyers seek to obtain the best product or service at the most reasonable cost. Negotiation is the vehicle through which these objectives are met.

Relationship Building: Successful negotiations are not zero-sum games; they are opportunities to build trust and rapport. A salesperson who navigates negotiations with professionalism, fairness, and respect can leave a lasting positive impression on the buyer. This can lead to repeat business, referrals, and the foundation of a long-term customer relationship.

Overcoming Obstacles: Challenges and objections are common in sales. Negotiations provide a structured process for addressing these issues. By understanding the buyer's concerns and finding creative solutions, a skilled negotiator can turn objections into opportunities and remove barriers to a sale.

Customization: Negotiation allows for the customization of deals to meet the unique needs of each buyer. It enables sellers to offer tailored solutions that align with the buyer's specific requirements. This personalization can be a key factor in winning the deal over competitors with one-size-fits-all approaches.

Profitability: Effective negotiations directly impact a company's profitability. A well-negotiated deal can increase profit margins by securing higher prices, better terms, and cost-saving concessions. This boost to the bottom line is essential for a company's financial success.

Competitive Advantage: In a competitive market, the ability to negotiate effectively can be a significant differentiator. Buyers are more likely to choose a seller who can meet their needs and expectations during negotiations. This competitive advantage can lead to increased market share and revenue.

Risk Mitigation: Negotiations also serve to manage risk. Contracts and agreements negotiated with care and attention to detail can help protect both parties from potential disputes or misunderstandings down the road. This risk mitigation is crucial for maintaining a positive business relationship.

Market Dynamics: Market conditions can change rapidly, and negotiations allow sellers to adapt to these shifts. Whether it's adjusting pricing strategies, offering incentives, or accommodating changing buyer demands, negotiations enable sellers to remain agile in a dynamic marketplace.

Continuous Improvement: Through negotiations, sales professionals can gather valuable feedback about their products, services, and customer needs. This information can inform future sales strategies, product development, and business growth.

In conclusion, negotiations are the lifeblood of sales. They are the means by which deals are closed, value is maximized, relationships are built, and companies achieve profitability and growth. Effective negotiation skills are a critical asset for any salesperson or organization, and their significance in the sales process cannot be overstated. Those who master the art of negotiation have a competitive edge and the ability to thrive in the ever-evolving world of sales.

2.2 Case Study: Chris Voss - Mastering Negotiation Under Pressure

Background: Chris Voss, a former FBI hostage negotiator, is renowned for his expertise in high-stakes negotiations. His journey from the world of law enforcement to becoming a negotiation guru has provided valuable insights into the art of negotiating under extreme pressure.

Challenges: Chris faced the formidable challenge of negotiating with terrorists, criminals, and kidnappers during his tenure at the FBI. These situations required not only an understanding of negotiation principles but also the ability to remain calm, focused, and empathetic under the most intense pressure imaginable.

Strategy: Chris Voss developed a negotiation approach that has since become a cornerstone of his teachings. His strategies include:

Empathetic Listening: Understanding the emotional state and perspective of the other party is crucial. Voss emphasizes active listening to build rapport and trust even in life-threatening situations.

Tactical Empathy: This concept involves using empathy as a tactical advantage. By acknowledging the other party's emotions and needs, negotiators can influence outcomes and reduce resistance.

Mirroring and Labeling: Chris advocates mirroring the other party's words and labeling their emotions to create a sense of connection and openness. This technique helps in guiding the negotiation.

Calibrated Questions: Voss stresses the importance of asking open-ended questions that encourage the other party to share information and reveal their intentions.

Results: Chris Voss's approach to negotiation under pressure has yielded remarkable results:

Life-Saving Negotiations: His tactics have been instrumental in securing the release of hostages and resolving high-stakes crises, demonstrating the effectiveness of his methods even in life-and-death situations.

Cross-Industry Applications: Voss's negotiation principles extend beyond law enforcement, finding applications in business, diplomacy, and everyday interactions. His insights have helped professionals in various fields improve their negotiation skills.

Reduced Conflict: By emphasizing empathy and open communication, Voss's approach often leads to conflict resolution and mutually beneficial agreements, reducing the potential for violence or harm in high-pressure situations.

Teaching and Training: Chris Voss has become a sought-after speaker and trainer, sharing his expertise with organizations worldwide. His book, "Never Split the Difference," has become a bestseller and a valuable resource for negotiation enthusiasts.

Conclusion: Chris Voss's journey from an FBI hostage negotiator to a renowned negotiation expert showcases the significance of mastering negotiation under extreme pressure. His innovative strategies, rooted in empathy and effective communication, have not only saved lives but also transformed the way people approach negotiations in various domains. Voss's case study serves as a testament to the power of empathy, active listening, and tactical thinking in navigating high-stakes negotiations successfully, even when the pressure is at its peak.

2.3 Overcoming Common Negotiation Challenges

Negotiation is an essential skill in various aspects of life, from business deals to personal relationships. However, it's not without its challenges. Successfully navigating these obstacles can be the difference between a win-win agreement and a stalemate. Here are some common negotiation challenges and strategies to overcome them:

Emotional Attachments: Challenge: Emotions can cloud judgment and lead to irrational decision-making during negotiations. Strategy: Acknowledge and manage your emotions. Take breaks if needed to regain composure. Encourage the other party to do the same to maintain a rational atmosphere.

Lack of Information: Challenge: Negotiating without adequate information can weaken your position. Strategy: Prioritize research and preparation. Gather data, understand the other party's perspective, and anticipate their needs. Knowledge is a powerful tool in negotiations.

Communication Barriers: Challenge: Miscommunication or language barriers can lead to misunderstandings and conflict. Strategy: Practice active listening. Clarify any ambiguous points and encourage the other party to do the same. Use simple and clear language, especially in complex negotiations.

Deadlock or Impasse: Challenge: Stalemates can occur when both parties are unwilling to compromise. Strategy: Explore alternative solutions. Brainstorm creative options that could satisfy both parties' interests. Consider concessions that don't undermine your core objectives.

Overcoming Anchoring Effects: Challenge: The first offer often sets the tone for negotiations, and it can be challenging to overcome initial anchors. Strategy: Counteroffer strategically. Instead of rejecting or accepting the anchor outright, propose a well-reasoned counteroffer that considers both parties' interests. Be prepared to justify your position.

Difficult Personalities: Challenge: Dealing with difficult or aggressive negotiators can be stressful. Strategy: Stay calm and maintain professionalism. Focus on the issues at hand rather than reacting to personal attacks. Use active listening and empathy to defuse tense situations.

Time Constraints: Challenge: Negotiations can be time-consuming, and deadlines may loom. Strategy: Prioritize your objectives and concessions. Set clear time limits for each negotiation phase. Be open about deadlines to encourage a sense of urgency without rushing the process.

Negotiation Fatigue: Challenge: Prolonged negotiations can lead to exhaustion and diminished decision-making abilities. Strategy: Take breaks to recharge and refocus. Ensure both parties remain engaged and committed to reaching a resolution. Consider seeking mediation or involving fresh perspectives if negotiations stall.

Cultural Differences: Challenge: Negotiating across cultures can lead to misunderstandings and misinterpretations. Strategy: Research and understand cultural nuances. Show respect for the other party's cultural norms and be open to learning from each other's perspectives. Consider using cultural experts or interpreters when necessary.

Failure to Build Rapport: Challenge: Building trust and rapport can be difficult, particularly in high-stakes negotiations. Strategy: Invest time in relationship-building. Find common ground, share information, and demonstrate sincerity. Building trust can lead to more constructive and cooperative negotiations.

In conclusion, overcoming common negotiation challenges requires a combination of preparation, emotional intelligence, adaptability, and effective communication. By recognizing and addressing these challenges proactively, negotiators can increase their chances of reaching mutually beneficial agreements and fostering positive long-term relationships.

The Science of Persuasion: Winning Hearts and Minds

3.1 The Psychology of Persuasion in Sales

Sales is not just about presenting products or services; it's about understanding and leveraging the psychology of persuasion to influence buying decisions. Successful sales professionals recognize that human psychology plays a crucial role in convincing customers to say "yes." Here's a deeper look into the psychology of persuasion in sales:

1. Building Trust: Trust is the foundation of any successful sale. Buyers are more likely to make a purchase when they trust the seller. This trust can be established through factors such as credibility, reliability, and authenticity. Salespeople should focus on being honest, reliable, and consistent in their interactions.

2. Social Proof: People tend to follow the crowd. Sales can be influenced by showcasing positive testimonials, reviews, or endorsements from satisfied customers. When potential buyers see others who have had a positive experience, it creates a sense of safety and credibility.

3. Scarcity and Urgency: The fear of missing out is a powerful motivator. Sales professionals often use scarcity and urgency techniques to persuade buyers. Limited-time offers, low-stock alerts, and exclusive deals create a sense of urgency, encouraging customers to take action quickly.

4. Reciprocity: The principle of reciprocity suggests that people are more likely to give when they have received something. Offering value upfront, such as free trials, samples, or valuable information, can create a sense of indebtedness in the customer. They may be more inclined to reciprocate by making a purchase.

5. Anchoring and Pricing Psychology: The way prices are presented can significantly influence buying decisions. Anchoring involves presenting a higher-priced option first to make subsequent options seem more reasonable. Additionally, using pricing tactics like "99 cents" instead of "round" numbers can make a product or service appear cheaper.

6. Storytelling: Human beings are naturally drawn to stories. Sales professionals who can weave a compelling narrative around their product or service can engage customers on an emotional level. Stories create connections and can help customers visualize how the product or service fits into their lives.

7. Framing and Perception: How information is framed can impact how it is perceived. Positive framing emphasizes the benefits of a product or service, while negative framing highlights the consequences of not making a purchase. The way a message is framed can significantly influence a buyer's decision-making process.

8. Consistency and Commitment: People tend to act in ways that are consistent with their previous actions and commitments. Sales professionals can leverage this by getting small commitments from customers early in the process, such as signing up for a newsletter or attending a webinar. Once someone has committed to a small action, they are more likely to commit to a larger one, like making a purchase.

9. Emotional Appeal: Emotions often drive buying decisions more than logic. Salespeople who can tap into customers' emotions and show how their product or service can solve a problem, fulfill a desire, or make life better are more likely to be persuasive.

In conclusion, understanding the psychology of persuasion is a fundamental skill in sales. Sales professionals who recognize and utilize these psychological principles ethically and effectively are better equipped to influence buying decisions and build long-term customer relationships. By combining product knowledge with an understanding of human behavior, salespeople can become persuasive advocates for their offerings.

3.2 Case Study: Steve Jobs - The Master of Persuasion

Background: Steve Jobs, the co-founder of Apple Inc., is widely regarded as one of the most influential and persuasive leaders in the history of technology and business. His journey from a college dropout to a visionary entrepreneur showcases his exceptional ability to persuade and inspire.

Challenges: Throughout his career, Steve Jobs faced numerous challenges, including competition from established giants, product development setbacks, and the need to continually innovate in a rapidly changing industry. His success hinged on his capacity to persuade investors, employees, and customers to believe in his vision.

Strategies: Steve Jobs employed several strategies that set him apart as a master of persuasion:

Visionary Storytelling: Jobs had an uncanny ability to paint a vivid picture of the future. He used storytelling to convey his vision for groundbreaking products like the iPhone and iPad, making them seem not just revolutionary but essential to consumers' lives.

Passion and Belief: Jobs exuded passion for his products and an unwavering belief in their transformative potential. His enthusiasm was infectious, rallying employees, partners, and customers around a shared sense of purpose.

Simplicity and Design: Jobs understood the power of simplicity and aesthetics in persuasion. He championed minimalist design and user-friendly interfaces, making Apple products not only functional but also emotionally appealing.

Product Demonstrations: Jobs was a master of product demonstrations. He would unveil Apple's latest innovations with theatrical flair, showcasing their features, benefits, and ease of use. These presentations built anticipation and desire among the audience.

Creating Desire through Scarcity: By carefully managing product releases and creating an aura of exclusivity, Jobs generated a sense of scarcity and urgency around Apple products, driving demand to unparalleled levels.

Results: Steve Jobs's mastery of persuasion yielded remarkable results:

Loyal Customer Base: Apple cultivated a fiercely loyal customer base that eagerly awaited each new product release, often standing in line for hours to be among the first to own the latest Apple device.

Market Dominance: Under Jobs's leadership, Apple became one of the world's most valuable companies, with products like the iPhone and iPad revolutionizing their respective industries.

Innovation Legacy: Jobs's persuasive abilities led to the creation of groundbreaking technologies and the establishment of Apple as a global innovation leader.

Inspiration: His persuasive storytelling inspired countless entrepreneurs and business leaders to strive for excellence and aim for transformative impact.

Conclusion: Steve Jobs's exceptional talent for persuasion transcended product features and functionalities. He tapped into the emotional and aspirational aspects of his audience's psyche, creating a lasting legacy that continues to influence the world of technology and design. His case serves as a testament to the power of persuasion in business leadership and the enduring impact it can have on industries and consumers alike.

3.3 Crafting Persuasive Sales Pitches

Creating crafty sales pitches is both an art and a science. It involves more than just presenting product features; it's about engaging your audience, addressing their needs, and compelling them to take action. Here are some key strategies for crafting persuasive sales pitches:

Know Your Audience: Tailor your pitch to the specific needs, preferences, and pain points of your audience. Research your prospects to understand their demographics, motivations, and challenges. A pitch that resonates with the audience's desires is more likely to capture their attention.

Start with a Hook: Begin your pitch with a compelling hook—a captivating story, a startling statistic, or a thought-provoking question. The opening should grab your audience's attention and pique their curiosity.

Highlight Benefits, Not Just Features: While features are important, emphasize how your product or service benefits the customer. Explain how it can solve their problems, make their lives easier, or enhance their experiences. Paint a vivid picture of the positive outcomes they can expect.

Create a Sense of Urgency: Incorporate a time-sensitive element to encourage immediate action. Limited-time offers, special promotions, or the fear of missing out (FOMO) can motivate prospects to make a decision sooner rather than later.

Use Social Proof: Share success stories, testimonials, and case studies to demonstrate how others have benefited from your offering. People tend to trust the experiences of their peers, making social proof a powerful persuasion tool.

Address Objections Proactively: Anticipate and address potential objections or concerns your prospects may have. By acknowledging and providing solutions to their doubts, you demonstrate transparency and build trust.

Demonstrate Value: Showcase the unique value proposition of your product or service. Highlight what sets you apart from the competition and why choosing your offering is the best decision.

Engage in Two-Way Communication: A crafty pitch is not a monologue; it's a conversation. Encourage questions and interaction. Listen actively to your prospects, show empathy, and adjust your pitch accordingly.

Visual Aids and Storytelling: Use visual aids, such as charts, graphs, or compelling images, to reinforce your message. Additionally, storytelling can help illustrate the benefits of your product or service in a relatable and memorable way.

Practice and Refine: Crafting a compelling sales pitch takes practice. Role-play with colleagues or mentors to refine your pitch. Continuously seek feedback and make adjustments based on what works best.

Follow Up: After delivering your pitch, follow up promptly with prospects to answer any remaining questions and reinforce your message. Consistent follow-up demonstrates your commitment and interest in their needs.

In conclusion, crafty sales pitches combine persuasive techniques with a deep understanding of your audience. By engaging your prospects, addressing their concerns, and highlighting the value of your offering, you can create pitches that not only capture attention but also drive action and close deals effectively. The art of persuasion in sales is a dynamic skill that evolves with practice and adaptability.

Conclusion: The Art and Science of Sales Mastery

Mastering sales skills is a multifaceted journey that requires continuous learning, practice, and adaptation. Building relationships, negotiation, and persuasion are the cornerstones of sales mastery, and case studies of successful salespeople offer valuable insights into applying these skills effectively. By honing these skills and principles, individuals and organizations can thrive in the competitive world of sales, driving growth, and achieving remarkable results.

Chapter 8: Sales Techniques and Strategies

The world of sales is dynamic and ever-evolving, but the foundations of effective sales techniques often find their roots in classic and modern literature. In this chapter, we will explore how timeless principles from literature can be applied to navigate the sales process successfully. By drawing inspiration from both classic and contemporary works, sales professionals can gain valuable insights and enhance their sales skills.

The Power of Persuasion in Classic Literature

Classic literature has long been celebrated for its ability to delve into the depths of human nature, portraying the complexities of human interactions, including the art of persuasion. Throughout the centuries, iconic literary works have explored the various facets of persuasion, its ethical implications, and its profound impact on characters and plot development. Here, we delve into the power of persuasion as portrayed in classic literature.

1. Jane Austen's "Pride and Prejudice": In this beloved novel, persuasion plays a central role in the courtship of Elizabeth Bennet and Mr. Darcy. Characters employ persuasion to win over hearts and minds, revealing the influence of social status, reputation, and genuine affection in the art of persuasion.

2. William Shakespeare's "Othello": Iago's masterful manipulation of Othello is a quintessential example of persuasion's dark side. Through cunning rhetoric and the exploitation of Othello's vulnerabilities, Iago persuades him to believe in baseless suspicions, leading to tragic consequences.

3. George Orwell's "1984": In this dystopian masterpiece, the totalitarian regime employs the power of persuasion to control its citizens' thoughts and beliefs. The concept of "Newspeak" highlights how language manipulation can be used as a tool of oppression and psychological control.

4. Homer's "The Odyssey": The cunning and persuasive skills of the character Odysseus are showcased as he navigates his way through a series of challenges and obstacles on his journey home. His persuasive abilities often prove to be more valuable than physical strength.

5. Charles Dickens's "Great Expectations": In this novel, the character Estella serves as a living embodiment of the power of persuasion. Her beauty and charm are used to manipulate Pip's emotions and desires, demonstrating how persuasion can be both enchanting and deceptive.

6. F. Scott Fitzgerald's "The Great Gatsby": Jay Gatsby's relentless pursuit of Daisy Buchanan exemplifies the theme of persuasion and the allure of the American Dream. Gatsby's persuasive persona and lavish parties are ultimately an attempt to win back the love of his life.

7. William Golding's "Lord of the Flies": The power of persuasion takes a dark turn in this novel as the character Jack uses fear and manipulation to sway the group of boys on the island. The novel explores the destructive potential of persuasion when it is driven by a thirst for power.

8. Mark Twain's "The Adventures of Huckleberry Finn": The friendship between Huck and Jim serves as a testament to the persuasive power of genuine human connection. Jim's kindness and wisdom gradually persuade Huck to question the prevailing racial prejudices of his society.

9. Mary Shelley's "Frankenstein": Victor Frankenstein's ability to persuade himself and others to pursue scientific endeavors has far-reaching consequences. The novel raises questions about the ethical boundaries of persuasion and scientific ambition.

10. Leo Tolstoy's "War and Peace": Tolstoy's epic novel delves into the power of persuasion within the context of Russian society during the Napoleonic Wars. Characters like Pierre Bezukhov undergo personal transformations influenced by persuasive philosophies and ideals.

In classic literature, the power of persuasion serves as a multifaceted lens through which authors explore themes of love, ambition, manipulation, and morality. These timeless works continue to resonate with readers, offering profound insights into the human condition and the enduring impact of persuasive words and actions. Classic literature reminds us that persuasion, whether used for good or ill, is a fundamental aspect of the human experience and a source of both triumph and tragedy in our stories.

Modern Sales Strategies Inspired by Literature

2.1 The Dale Carnegie Approach: Building Relationships

Dale Carnegie's timeless principles for building relationships have been a cornerstone of interpersonal success for decades. His approach, outlined in his iconic book "How to Win Friends and Influence People," emphasizes the importance of genuine, empathetic, and respectful interactions with others.

At its core, the Dale Carnegie Approach revolves around several key principles:

Show Genuine Interest: Carnegie advocates for showing sincere interest in others. By asking questions, actively listening, and seeking to understand their perspectives and interests, we can establish a strong foundation for meaningful relationships.

Give Compliments and Praise: Carnegie encourages the practice of offering honest and heartfelt compliments and praise. Recognizing others' contributions and achievements fosters goodwill and positive connections.

Be a Good Listener: Effective communication involves attentive listening. Carnegie stresses the importance of letting others talk and expressing genuine interest in their viewpoints, which builds trust and rapport.

Avoid Criticism and Condemnation: Carnegie advises against criticizing, condemning, or complaining about others. Instead, he encourages a constructive approach that seeks solutions rather than dwelling on problems.

Show Empathy: Understanding others' emotions and perspectives is crucial. Carnegie emphasizes the importance of empathy, which enables us to connect on a deeper level and support one another.

Make Others Feel Important: People appreciate feeling valued and significant. Carnegie's approach teaches us to make others feel important by acknowledging their contributions and showing appreciation.

Give Feedback Diplomatically: When providing feedback or addressing concerns, Carnegie recommends using diplomacy and tact. Constructive feedback should be offered in a way that preserves relationships and encourages improvement.

Smile and Be Approachable: A warm smile and a friendly demeanor can make a significant difference in how others perceive us. Carnegie encourages approachability and a positive attitude.

The Dale Carnegie Approach's enduring popularity lies in its emphasis on human connection and respect. By embracing these principles, individuals can build strong, authentic relationships that enhance their personal and professional lives. This approach reminds us that the foundation of success in any endeavor often rests on the quality of the relationships we cultivate with others.

2.2 Robert Cialdini's "Influence": The Psychology of Persuasion

Robert Cialdini's "Influence: The Psychology of Persuasion" is a seminal work that delves into the intricate mechanisms of human persuasion and the psychological triggers that lead people to say "yes." Cialdini's exploration of the psychology of influence has had a profound impact on fields such as marketing, sales, and psychology.

The book outlines six key principles of persuasion:

Reciprocity: People have a natural inclination to reciprocate when they receive a favor or gift. By offering something of value to others, whether it's a small gift or a helpful gesture, individuals can elicit a sense of indebtedness, increasing the likelihood of a favorable response.

Commitment and Consistency: Once people make a commitment or take a stand, they tend to remain consistent with their initial choice. Cialdini explains how this principle can be harnessed to influence behavior by securing small commitments that pave the way for larger ones.

Social Proof: People often look to others for guidance when making decisions. Demonstrating that others have taken a particular action or endorsed a product or idea can be a powerful persuasive tool.

Authority: Cialdini explores how individuals tend to defer to authority figures and experts. Establishing one's credibility and expertise can significantly enhance persuasive efforts.

Liking: People are more inclined to say "yes" to those they know, like, and trust. Building rapport, finding common ground, and creating a connection with others can increase the chances of persuasion.

Scarcity: The fear of missing out drives people to act quickly. By highlighting the scarcity of a product or opportunity, individuals can create a sense of urgency, motivating others to take action.

"Influence" offers valuable insights into the subtle ways individuals are influenced in their decision-making processes. Cialdini's work has become a foundational text for marketers, salespeople, and anyone interested in understanding the psychology of persuasion. It underscores the importance of ethical and responsible persuasion, emphasizing the need to use these principles in ways that benefit both parties involved in the exchange.

2.3 Malcolm Gladwell's "The Tipping Point": Creating Sales Momentum

Malcolm Gladwell's "The Tipping Point" explores the concept of how ideas, trends, and behaviors reach a critical mass, triggering rapid and widespread adoption. While the book primarily focuses on societal phenomena, its principles can be applied to creating sales momentum.

In the context of sales, the tipping point represents that pivotal moment when a product or service gains significant traction and demand. Gladwell's book highlights the factors that contribute to this tipping point, including the roles of connectors (networkers), mavens (influencers), and salespeople (persuaders).

Sales professionals can leverage these insights by identifying connectors and mavens within their target markets. By building relationships with these individuals, they can amplify their messages and recommendations to reach a broader audience. Additionally, understanding the specific triggers that lead to the tipping point, such as word-of-mouth referrals or social validation, can inform sales strategies and help generate the momentum needed to drive sales success.

Navigating the Sales Process with Literary Wisdom

3.1 Sun Tzu's "The Art of War": Strategy in Sales

Sun Tzu's ancient treatise "The Art of War" may seem like an unconventional source of wisdom for sales, but its principles of strategy, competition, and maneuvering hold valuable insights for modern sales professionals. Here's how "The Art of War" can be applied to the world of sales:

Know Your Terrain (Market): Sun Tzu emphasizes the importance of understanding the battlefield. In sales, this translates to thorough market research. Sales professionals must know their industry, competition, target audience, and market trends inside and out.

Understand Your Enemy (Competitor): Sun Tzu's wisdom regarding understanding your adversary applies to understanding your competitors. Analyze their strengths and weaknesses, anticipate their moves, and position your product or service effectively.

The Importance of Strategy: Sun Tzu emphasizes the significance of strategy and planning. In sales, this involves crafting a well-thought-out sales strategy, setting clear goals, and developing tactics to achieve them.

Adaptability: Sun Tzu stresses the importance of adaptability. In sales, this means being flexible and adjusting your approach based on changing market conditions, customer feedback, and competition.

Leverage Your Strengths: Sun Tzu advises playing to your strengths and exploiting your competitor's weaknesses. Sales professionals should identify their unique selling points and use them to their advantage.

Deception and Misdirection: Sun Tzu discusses the use of deception and misdirection to gain an advantage. In sales, this can involve strategic positioning, marketing tactics, and presenting information in a compelling yet truthful manner.

Build Alliances: Sun Tzu advocates building alliances and partnerships. In sales, this means collaborating with complementary businesses, creating referral networks, and leveraging existing customer relationships for new opportunities.

Winning Without Fighting: Sun Tzu suggests that the best victory is one achieved without direct conflict. In sales, this can translate to successful negotiations, objection handling, and the art of persuasion, where customers feel like they are making the decision themselves.

Continuous Improvement: Sun Tzu's emphasis on self-improvement aligns with the need for ongoing skill development in sales. Continuous learning, refining sales techniques, and adapting to changing customer behaviors are crucial.

In conclusion, Sun Tzu's "The Art of War" offers strategic wisdom that can be applied to the competitive world of sales. While the battlefield may differ, the principles of understanding, strategy, adaptability, and continual improvement are timeless and can empower sales professionals to navigate their market successfully, outmaneuver competitors, and achieve their objectives.

3.2 George Orwell's "1984": Effective Communication

George Orwell's dystopian novel "1984" serves as a cautionary tale about the power of language, propaganda, and the manipulation of communication. It underscores the importance of effective communication in shaping perceptions and controlling societies.

In the novel, the totalitarian regime led by Big Brother employs the concept of "Newspeak" to manipulate and limit language. The government aims to control thought by eliminating words and concepts that might challenge its authority. This illustrates the idea that controlling language can control thought, and controlling thought can control actions.

The novel also highlights the impact of propaganda through slogans like "War is Peace," "Freedom is Slavery," and "Ignorance is Strength." These paradoxical statements are used to confuse and manipulate citizens, illustrating the power of language to distort reality.

"1984" serves as a stark reminder of the importance of clear and honest communication in maintaining a free and just society. Effective communication is not just about conveying information; it is about fostering understanding, critical thinking, and open discourse. In a world where language is weaponized for control, the novel emphasizes the need to safeguard the principles of truth, transparency, and free expression in our own communication to preserve democratic values and individual freedom

Case Studies: Applying Literary Wisdom to Real Sales Scenarios

4.1 Case Study: Selling Luxury with Shakespearean Eloquence

Background: In the world of luxury goods, where exclusivity, elegance, and allure are paramount, a unique approach to sales is required. One such approach involves leveraging the timeless eloquence and poetic charm of William Shakespeare's literary genius to sell luxury products.

Strategy: A luxury brand seeking to differentiate itself in a competitive market decided to adopt a Shakespearean-inspired approach. They incorporated elements of Shakespearean language, themes, and aesthetics into their marketing and sales strategies.

1. The Power of Language: The brand's marketing materials and sales pitches were crafted with rich, poetic language reminiscent of Shakespearean sonnets and soliloquies. This heightened language not only elevated the product descriptions but also created an emotional connection with potential customers.

2. Storytelling: Shakespearean plays are known for their compelling narratives. The brand incorporated storytelling into its marketing campaigns, linking its products to captivating tales of love, ambition, and beauty. This not only added depth to the brand's identity but also engaged customers on a deeper level.

3. Exclusive Experiences: Luxury brands often offer exclusive experiences to their clientele. The brand organized events and gatherings inspired by Shakespearean themes, allowing customers to immerse themselves in the elegance and artistry associated with the Bard's era.

4. Limited Editions: Just as Shakespeare's works endure as limited editions of literary excellence, the brand introduced limited-edition luxury products, tying them to the allure of exclusivity and rarity.

5. Artistic Collaborations: The brand collaborated with artists and designers inspired by Shakespearean motifs to create unique, high-end collections that resonated with Shakespearean aesthetics.

Results: The brand's innovative approach resulted in several notable outcomes:

Enhanced Brand Identity: The Shakespearean-inspired approach gave the brand a distinct and memorable identity in the luxury market,

Increased Engagement: Customers were drawn to the poetic language, storytelling, and exclusive experiences, leading to higher levels of engagement and brand loyalty.

Positive Perception: The brand was perceived as not just a purveyor of luxury goods but as a curator of art, culture, and elegance, further elevating its reputation.

Sales Growth: The unique approach attracted new customers and encouraged existing ones to explore the brand's offerings, ultimately leading to increased sales and revenue.

In conclusion, selling luxury with Shakespearean eloquence is a testament to the enduring power of timeless language, storytelling, and artistry. By infusing the elegance and charm of Shakespearean themes into their marketing and sales strategies, luxury brands can create a unique and enchanting experience for their clientele, fostering deeper connections and driving growth in an increasingly competitive market.

4.2 Case Study: Influencer Marketing a la Cialdini

Influencer marketing has become a prominent strategy for brands to reach and engage their target audiences. To optimize this approach, a company decided to integrate principles from Robert Cialdini's "Influence: The Psychology of Persuasion" into their influencer marketing campaign.

Strategy: The company sought to leverage Cialdini's persuasion principles to enhance the effectiveness of their influencer marketing:

1. Reciprocity: To tap into the principle of reciprocity, the brand encouraged influencers to offer their followers exclusive promotions, giveaways, or valuable content, creating a sense of indebtedness among the audience.

2. Social Proof: The company carefully selected influencers who already had a substantial following and strong engagement rates. This established social proof, demonstrating that their products or services were endorsed and appreciated by others.

3. Liking: The brand chose influencers whose values and persona aligned with their product, ensuring a genuine connection that resonated with the audience. This fostered a sense of liking and trust among followers.

4. Authority: The influencers were positioned as authorities in their respective niches, with expertise and credibility that aligned with the brand's offerings. This lent authority and credibility to the products or services being promoted.

Results: The incorporation of Cialdini's principles into influencer marketing yielded several positive outcomes:

Increased Engagement: The campaign saw a significant increase in engagement, as influencers effectively harnessed the principles of reciprocity, social proof, liking, and authority.

Improved Brand Perception: The brand was perceived as more trustworthy and credible due to its association with influencers who embodied Cialdini's principles.

Higher Conversion Rates: Influencer-driven content resulted in a notable boost in conversion rates, as followers were more inclined to take action based on the recommendations of influencers they admired.

Enhanced ROI: The influencer marketing campaign delivered a higher return on investment, thanks to the strategic application of persuasion principles.

In conclusion, incorporating Robert Cialdini's persuasion principles into influencer marketing can significantly enhance its impact and effectiveness. By carefully selecting influencers who embody these principles and aligning their messaging with Cialdini's concepts, brands can create more compelling, persuasive, and successful influencer marketing campaigns that resonate with their target audience.

Conclusion: The Literary Tapestry of Sales Mastery

Incorporating lessons from classic and modern literature into sales techniques adds depth and dimension to the art of selling. By understanding the psychology of persuasion, embracing effective communication, and navigating the sales process strategically, sales professionals can elevate their skills and achieve remarkable results. The timeless wisdom of literature serves as a valuable guide on the journey to sales mastery, where each page turned reveals new insights and opportunities for success

Chapter 9: Sales Leadership

In the competitive landscape of business, sales leadership plays a pivotal role in driving revenue, growth, and organizational success. Effective sales leadership goes beyond managing a team; it involves inspiring, coaching, and fostering a culture that is sales-driven. In this chapter, we will explore the essential aspects of sales leadership and how to cultivate a sales-driven culture within an organization.

Introduction: The Strategic Significance of Sales Leadership

Sales leadership plays a pivotal role in driving the success and growth of organizations across industries. It is the guiding force that shapes sales teams, influences customer relationships, and ultimately impacts the bottom line. In this era of rapidly evolving markets and customer expectations, the strategic significance of sales leadership cannot be overstated.

Effective sales leadership is not merely about overseeing sales teams; it encompasses the art of inspiring, motivating, and equipping sales professionals to excel. Sales leaders set the vision, establish goals, and design the strategies that steer their teams towards success. They foster a culture of innovation, resilience, and customer-centricity that ensures sustainable growth.

Furthermore, sales leaders are at the forefront of adapting to market dynamics, technological advancements, and changing customer behaviors. They must possess the skills to navigate complex negotiations, build lasting customer relationships, and drive revenue generation while staying agile in the face of challenges.

In this exploration of the strategic significance of sales leadership, we will delve into the multifaceted roles and responsibilities of sales leaders, their impact on organizational success, and the evolving landscape in which they operate. Effective sales leadership is the linchpin of a company's revenue engine, and its significance continues to grow as businesses seek to thrive in a competitive global marketplace.

The Characteristics of Effective Sales Leaders

Effective sales leaders possess a unique set of characteristics that enable them to inspire and guide their teams to success. These qualities form the foundation of their leadership style and contribute to a sales-driven culture.

2.1 Vision and Strategy

Effective sales leaders possess a clear vision and a strategic mindset. Their vision is a beacon that guides their team toward a shared goal, be it market dominance, customer satisfaction, or revenue growth. They craft a strategy that aligns resources, tactics, and goals, leveraging market insights, customer feedback, and emerging trends. This strategy is flexible yet disciplined, adapting to changing circumstances while staying true to the overarching vision. Effective sales leaders communicate this vision and strategy with enthusiasm, inspiring their team to work cohesively toward a common objective. They are agile and data-driven, ready to pivot when necessary but always focused on long-term success.

Key Attributes:

The ability to articulate a compelling vision for the sales team.

Crafting a sales strategy that aligns with organizational objectives.

Communicating the strategy to the team and ensuring buy-in.

2.2 Leading by Example

Leading by example is a fundamental trait of successful sales leaders. They set the standard for performance, work ethic, and professionalism, inspiring their teams to follow suit.

Exemplary Leadership:

Modeling the behavior and work ethic they expect from the team.

Demonstrating resilience and determination in the face of challenges.

Upholding the organization's values and ethical standards.

2.3 Empathy and Emotional Intelligence

Effective sales leaders possess high levels of empathy and emotional intelligence. They understand the needs and motivations of their team members, fostering a supportive and collaborative environment.

Empathy and Emotional Intelligence in Sales Leadership:

Recognizing and addressing the emotional needs of the sales team.

Creating a culture of trust and open communication.

Leveraging emotional intelligence to resolve conflicts and build strong relationships.

2.4 Accountability and Responsibility

Sales leaders take ownership of their team's performance and results. They hold themselves accountable for both successes and setbacks, driving a culture of responsibility within the sales organization.

Accountability and Responsibility in Sales Leadership:

Setting clear expectations and performance standards.

Acknowledging mistakes and learning from them.

Encouraging a sense of ownership among team members.

2.5 Continuous Learning and Adaptability

Sales leaders understand that the business landscape is constantly evolving. They prioritize continuous learning, staying updated on industry trends and emerging technologies, and adapt their strategies accordingly.

Commitment to Learning and Adaptation:

Seeking opportunities for professional development.

Embracing change and innovation in sales processes.

Encouraging the sales team to embrace a growth mindset.

Building a Sales-Driven Culture

A sales-driven culture is one where the entire organization recognizes the importance of sales and actively supports the sales team's efforts. It involves aligning every department with the goal of driving revenue and fostering collaboration across the organization.

3.1 Communicating the Sales Vision

Sales leaders play a critical role in communicating the sales vision to the entire organization. They ensure that every employee understands the significance of sales and how their role contributes to revenue generation.

Effective Communication of the Sales Vision:

Consistently communicating the sales strategy and objectives.

Highlighting the impact of sales on the organization's growth.

Celebrating sales achievements and milestones with the entire team.

3.2 Collaboration Across Departments

A sales-driven culture thrives on collaboration between sales and other departments, such as marketing, product development, and customer service. Sales leaders foster a sense of unity and shared purpose.

Cross-Functional Collaboration:

Encouraging regular communication and collaboration with other departments.

Aligning marketing efforts with sales objectives to generate high-quality leads.

Sharing customer feedback and insights to drive product improvements.

3.3 Sales Training and Development

Investing in the training and development of the sales team is a cornerstone of a sales-driven culture. Sales leaders ensure that team members have the skills and knowledge needed to excel in their roles.

Sales Training and Development Initiatives:

Providing ongoing sales training and coaching.

Supporting certifications and skill enhancement programs.

Recognizing and rewarding continuous improvement in sales skills.

3.4 Metrics and Performance Measurement

Measuring and analyzing sales performance is essential for a sales-driven culture. Sales leaders establish key performance indicators (KPIs) and use data-driven insights to make informed decisions.

Data-Driven Sales Culture:

Setting clear, measurable KPIs for the sales team.

Regularly reviewing and analyzing sales data to identify trends and opportunities.

Using performance metrics to guide strategic adjustments and improvements.

Case Studies: Leading Sales Teams and Cultivating Sales-Driven Cultures

4.1 Case Study: Salesforce - A Culture of Customer-Centric Selling

Salesforce, a leading CRM provider, has cultivated a sales-driven culture centered around customer success. Sales leaders prioritize customer satisfaction and ensure that every team member understands their role in delivering value to clients.

Key Takeaways:

Aligning sales objectives with customer success.

Providing extensive training and resources for the sales team.

Emphasizing the importance of customer feedback and retention.

4.2 Case Study: HubSpot - Inbound Sales Excellence

HubSpot, a leading provider of inbound marketing and sales software, has become synonymous with inbound sales excellence. The company's innovative approach to sales and customer engagement has transformed the way businesses attract, engage, and delight customers.

Strategy: HubSpot's inbound sales strategy revolves around a few key principles:

1. Customer-Centricity: HubSpot places the customer at the center of its strategy. Rather than relying on traditional outbound sales tactics, HubSpot focuses on creating valuable content and experiences that attract and engage prospects.

2. Content Marketing: HubSpot's extensive library of educational content, including blogs, webinars, e-books, and more, not only positions the company as an industry authority but also serves as a powerful lead generation tool.

3. Personalization: HubSpot leverages data and technology to personalize interactions with prospects and customers. Their CRM system enables sales teams to have meaningful, tailored conversations with each lead.

4. Sales Enablement: HubSpot provides its sales teams with tools and resources to excel. Sales professionals are equipped with data-driven insights, automation, and analytics to optimize their efforts.

5. Continuous Learning: HubSpot invests in training and development for its sales teams, ensuring they stay up-to-date with industry trends and best practices in inbound sales.

Results: HubSpot's inbound sales excellence has yielded remarkable results:

Rapid Growth: The company has experienced rapid growth, expanding its customer base globally and consistently exceeding revenue expectations.

Customer Loyalty: HubSpot's customer-centric approach has earned the loyalty of thousands of businesses who trust the platform to fuel their growth.

Industry Influence: HubSpot's thought leadership in inbound marketing and sales has shaped industry practices and inspired countless businesses to adopt similar approaches.

Employee Satisfaction: The company's focus on employee development and well-being has resulted in high employee satisfaction and a motivated workforce.

In conclusion, HubSpot's commitment to inbound sales excellence has not only positioned the company as a leader in the marketing and sales software industry but has also set a benchmark for customer-centricity and innovative sales strategies. This case study underscores the significance of inbound sales in today's business landscape and the transformative impact it can have on an organization's growth and success.

4.3 Case Study: Amazon - Data-Driven Sales Leadership

Amazon, the e-commerce giant founded by Jeff Bezos, is a prime example of data-driven sales leadership. The company's relentless focus on leveraging data to inform decision-making has played a pivotal role in its success.

Strategy: Amazon's data-driven sales leadership strategy includes:

1. Personalized Recommendations: Amazon uses algorithms and customer data to provide highly personalized product recommendations, increasing cross-selling and upselling opportunities.

2. Inventory Management: The company uses data analytics to optimize inventory levels, ensuring products are available when and where customers want them while minimizing carrying costs.

3. Pricing Optimization: Amazon adjusts product prices dynamically based on real-time market data, competitive pricing, and customer behavior to maximize sales and profitability.

4. Customer Insights: Through data analysis, Amazon gains insights into customer preferences, allowing them to tailor marketing campaigns, promotions, and product offerings.

5. Forecasting and Demand Planning: Advanced analytics help Amazon forecast demand with precision, reducing stockouts and overstocking.

Results: Amazon's data-driven sales leadership has delivered impressive outcomes:

Market Dominance: Amazon is one of the world's largest e-commerce platforms, with a substantial share of the online retail market.

Revenue Growth: Data-driven decisions have led to consistent revenue growth, making Amazon one of the most valuable companies globally.

Customer Satisfaction: Personalized experiences and efficient operations have contributed to high levels of customer satisfaction and loyalty.

Operational Efficiency: Amazon's use of data has optimized its supply chain and logistics operations, improving overall efficiency and reducing costs.

In conclusion, Amazon's data-driven sales leadership exemplifies the profound impact data analytics can have on sales strategy, customer satisfaction, and overall business success. By harnessing the power of data, Amazon continues to shape the future of e-commerce and redefine the standards for data-driven decision-making in sales.

Conclusion: The Impact of Sales Leadership on Organizational Success

Sales leadership is not confined to the sales team alone; it permeates every aspect of an organization. Effective sales leaders possess the qualities and vision to inspire their teams and cultivate a sales-driven culture that extends throughout the entire organization. By prioritizing traits like vision, empathy, accountability, and adaptability, sales leaders can lead their teams to achieve remarkable results and drive sustainable growth. The success of an organization often hinges on the strength of its sales leadership and the culture it fosters, making it a critical component of long-term success in the competitive business landscape.

Chapter 10: Sales and Business Growth

Sales and business growth share an intricate relationship that is fundamental to the success of any organization. Sales, often viewed as the lifeblood of a company, drives revenue and fuels expansion. In this chapter, we will explore the dynamic interplay between sales and business growth, examining how effective sales strategies, customer-centric approaches, and the measurement of sales effectiveness contribute to an organization's sustainable growth.

The Role of Sales in Business Growth

1.1 Revenue Generation

Revenue generation is a pivotal role of sales in driving business growth. Sales teams are at the forefront of a company's efforts to turn prospects into paying customers, thereby increasing the top line. This revenue not only fuels immediate growth but also provides resources for further expansion and innovation.

Sales professionals identify and pursue opportunities in the market, convert leads into customers, and maximize the value of existing accounts. Their efforts directly impact a company's financial health, allowing it to invest in product development, marketing, infrastructure, and talent acquisition.

Furthermore, a well-executed sales strategy can lead to sustainable revenue growth by fostering customer loyalty and repeat business. Sales teams play a critical role in understanding customer needs, providing tailored solutions, and building lasting relationships, all of which contribute to long-term revenue streams.

In essence, sales is the lifeblood of a business, and effective revenue generation is essential for achieving and sustaining growth. It ensures the financial stability and viability of an organization while enabling it to adapt, innovate, and thrive in a competitive marketplace.

1.2 Market Expansion

Market expansion is a crucial role of sales in driving business growth. Sales teams are responsible for identifying and tapping into new markets, both domestically and internationally, to broaden a company's reach and customer base.

Sales professionals conduct market research to identify emerging opportunities, assess market potential, and understand the needs of potential customers. They develop market entry strategies, establish partnerships, and create tailored sales approaches to penetrate new territories effectively.

Expanding into new markets allows a company to diversify its customer base, reduce dependence on specific regions, and capture additional revenue streams. It also enhances a company's resilience to economic fluctuations in particular markets.

Furthermore, market expansion opens doors to untapped demographics, industries, and customer segments, providing opportunities for increased sales and market share. When executed successfully, market expansion contributes significantly to a company's overall growth, driving revenue, profitability, and long-term sustainability in an ever-evolving business landscape.

1.3 Customer Acquisition

Customer acquisition is a central role of sales in driving business growth. Sales teams are tasked with identifying, targeting, and converting potential customers into paying clients. This process is essential for expanding a company's customer base, increasing revenue, and fueling overall growth.

Sales professionals use a range of strategies, including prospecting, lead generation, and outreach, to identify potential customers who align with the company's products or services. They leverage their knowledge of the market, competitive landscape, and customer needs to craft compelling pitches and value propositions that resonate with prospects.

Effective customer acquisition strategies involve building rapport, nurturing relationships, and addressing customer pain points. Sales teams not only convert leads into customers but also lay the foundation for ongoing engagement and customer loyalty.

Moreover, customer acquisition is not a one-time effort; it's an ongoing process that contributes to sustainable growth. It involves continuously adapting sales techniques, leveraging data and analytics, and aligning with evolving market trends.

Successful customer acquisition not only boosts revenue but also strengthens a company's market presence and competitive advantage. It is a vital component of any growth strategy, enabling businesses to expand their reach, increase market share, and ultimately thrive in a competitive business landscape.

Customer-Centric Sales Strategies

2.1 Building Customer Relationships

Long-term growth depends on nurturing strong customer relationships. Sales professionals must prioritize customer satisfaction and retention.

Strategies for Relationship Building:

Effective relationship building is at the core of successful sales. Here are key strategies for nurturing strong, lasting customer relationships:

Active Listening: Truly understand your customer's needs and concerns by actively listening to them. Show empathy and ask clarifying questions to demonstrate your commitment to their success.

Personalization: Tailor your interactions and solutions to each customer's unique needs. Personalization shows that you value them as individuals, not just as transactions.

Consistent Communication: Stay in touch regularly but not intrusively. Provide valuable insights, updates, and support to maintain a meaningful connection.

Transparency: Be open and honest in your dealings. Transparency builds trust, a critical element of any lasting relationship.

Underpromise, Overdeliver: Set realistic expectations and then strive to exceed them. This approach consistently delights customers and reinforces their trust in your reliability.

Anticipate Needs: Proactively identify potential pain points or opportunities for your customers and offer solutions before they even ask.

Post-Sale Care: Your relationship doesn't end with the sale. Continue to provide support, address concerns, and seek feedback to ensure ongoing satisfaction.

Face Challenges Together: When issues arise, face them head-on and work collaboratively to find solutions. Customers appreciate vendors who are willing to take responsibility and resolve problems.

Celebrate Successes: Acknowledge milestones and achievements in your customer's journey. Celebrating together fosters a sense of partnership.

Seek Feedback: Regularly solicit feedback to understand how you can improve and better serve your customers. Act on their input to demonstrate your commitment to their satisfaction.

By implementing these strategies, sales professionals can build strong, trust-based relationships that not only lead to increased customer loyalty but also generate referrals and long-term business growth

2.2 Customer-Centric Selling

Customer-centric selling focuses on understanding and addressing customer pain points. It emphasizes creating value for the customer rather than simply making a sale.

Customer-Centric Selling Approaches:

In customer-centric selling:

Understanding Customer Needs: Sales professionals take the time to truly understand the customer's challenges, goals, and pain points. They actively listen and ask probing questions to uncover underlying needs.

Tailored Solutions: Instead of offering a one-size-fits-all solution, customer-centric selling involves customizing offerings to meet the customer's specific requirements. This may involve bundling products or services, adjusting pricing, or modifying features.

Building Trust: By prioritizing the customer's best interests, salespeople build trust. Customers feel that the salesperson genuinely cares about their success, which leads to stronger relationships and repeat business.

Long-Term Focus: Customer-centric selling looks beyond the immediate sale. Sales professionals aim to create loyal customers who return for future purchases and become advocates for the brand.

Feedback and Improvement: Customer feedback is actively sought and used to improve products, services, and the overall sales process.

Customer-centric selling not only enhances customer satisfaction and loyalty but also drives revenue growth. It aligns with the modern customer's desire for personalized experiences and solutions tailored to their unique needs, making it a valuable approach in today's competitive business landscape.

2.3 Customer Lifetime Value (CLV)

Understanding CLV is essential for sustainable growth. Sales teams should focus on not only acquiring customers but also maximizing their lifetime value to the company.

CLV Enhancement Strategies:

Customer Lifetime Value (CLV) strategies are essential for businesses seeking sustainable growth and profitability. CLV represents the total revenue a customer is expected to generate throughout their relationship with a company. Here are key strategies for optimizing CLV:

Customer Segmentation: Identify customer segments based on behavior, demographics, and purchase history. Tailor marketing and communication to each segment's preferences and needs.

Personalization: Use data-driven insights to offer personalized recommendations, content, and promotions that resonate with individual customers, fostering loyalty.

Excellent Customer Service: Provide exceptional customer support to ensure a positive experience. Satisfied customers are more likely to return and refer others.

Customer Retention Programs: Implement loyalty programs, exclusive offers, and incentives to encourage repeat purchases and long-term engagement.

Upselling and Cross-Selling: Recommend complementary products or upgrades to increase the average transaction value over time.

Feedback and Improvement: Continuously seek feedback from customers to enhance products and services, demonstrating a commitment to their satisfaction.

Predictive Analytics: Utilize predictive analytics to forecast future CLV and identify high-value customer prospects for targeted marketing efforts.

Referral Programs: Encourage satisfied customers to refer friends and family, expanding your customer base through word-of-mouth.

Subscription Models: Offer subscription-based services or products to secure recurring revenue streams.

Quality Assurance: Consistently deliver high-quality products and services to maintain trust and satisfaction, ensuring customers stay engaged for the long haul.

By implementing these strategies, businesses can not only increase CLV but also cultivate strong, loyal customer relationships that drive sustained growth and profitability over time.

Measuring Sales Effectiveness

3.1 Key Performance Indicators (KPIs)

Measuring Key Performance Indicators (KPIs) in sales is of paramount importance because it provides a comprehensive understanding of a sales team's effectiveness and progress toward achieving its goals. Here's why KPI measurement is crucial in sales:

Performance Evaluation: KPIs allow sales managers and leaders to assess individual and team performance. They help identify top performers, areas for improvement, and coaching opportunities.

Goal Achievement: Sales KPIs are directly tied to sales targets and revenue goals. Measuring KPIs ensures that the team is on track to meet or exceed these objectives, providing early warning if targets are at risk.

Sales Process Optimization: KPIs shed light on every stage of the sales process, from lead generation to conversion. This data helps refine strategies, identify bottlenecks, and optimize the sales funnel for better efficiency.

Resource Allocation: By measuring KPIs, organizations can allocate resources effectively. This includes assigning leads to the right salespeople, investing in training where needed, and adjusting territories or market focus.

Motivation and Accountability: KPIs create a sense of accountability among sales professionals. They motivate teams to strive for excellence and encourage healthy competition.

Continuous Improvement: KPI measurement provides actionable insights for continuous improvement. Whether it's refining sales scripts, enhancing product knowledge, or streamlining follow-up processes, KPIs guide efforts to become more effective over time.

Strategic Decision-Making: Data-driven KPIs inform strategic decisions, such as pricing adjustments, product development, or market expansion. They provide a solid foundation for strategic planning.

In the competitive world of sales, measuring KPIs is not just about tracking performance; it's about ensuring that sales teams are aligned with organizational goals, optimizing processes, and constantly working toward higher levels of success. It's an essential practice for driving revenue growth and sustaining a thriving sales organization.

3.2 Sales Analytics

Firstly, it provides valuable insights into the performance of sales teams and individual representatives. By analyzing data on sales activities, conversions, and revenue, organizations can identify top performers, areas for improvement, and coaching needs.

Secondly, sales analytics enables data-driven decision-making. Sales leaders can make informed choices regarding pricing strategies, product offerings, and target markets based on market trends and customer behaviors.

Moreover, sales analytics aids in forecasting and goal setting. By examining historical data, organizations can set realistic sales targets and anticipate future revenue streams, allowing for better resource allocation and planning.

Furthermore, it helps in optimizing sales processes. By identifying bottlenecks or inefficiencies in the sales funnel, businesses can streamline operations, reduce costs, and improve overall efficiency.

Lastly, sales analytics enhances customer relationships. It allows organizations to understand customer preferences, tailor offerings, and provide personalized experiences, ultimately fostering loyalty and long-term relationships.

In conclusion, sales analytics is essential for driving growth, improving performance, and staying competitive in today's data-driven business environment. It empowers organizations to make informed decisions, optimize operations, and deliver superior value to customers.

3.3 Sales Technology

Sales technology offers a multitude of benefits that empower sales teams and organizations to thrive in a rapidly evolving business landscape. Here are some key advantages:

Efficiency and Productivity: Sales technology automates routine tasks, such as data entry, lead scoring, and follow-ups, allowing sales professionals to focus on high-value activities like building relationships and closing deals.

Data-Driven Insights: Sales technology provides real-time analytics and reporting, offering valuable insights into customer behavior, sales performance, and market trends. This data informs strategic decision-making and helps refine sales strategies.

Improved Lead Management: Advanced CRM systems and lead scoring tools help prioritize leads based on their potential, enabling sales teams to allocate resources more effectively and increase conversion rates.

Enhanced Customer Engagement: Sales technology facilitates personalized communication and outreach, which leads to stronger customer relationships and higher customer satisfaction.

Sales Forecasting: Accurate forecasting tools enable organizations to predict future sales and revenue, aiding in resource allocation, budgeting, and goal setting.

Remote Selling Capabilities: In an increasingly remote world, sales technology provides the tools and platforms necessary for effective virtual selling, ensuring that sales teams can adapt to changing market conditions.

Competitive Advantage: Organizations that embrace sales technology gain a competitive edge by staying ahead of the curve and delivering a superior customer experience.

Scalability: Sales technology is scalable, accommodating the needs of businesses of all sizes. It can grow with the organization, supporting expansion and increased sales volumes.

In conclusion, sales technology streamlines processes, enhances customer engagement, provides valuable insights, and contributes to increased sales and revenue. It is an essential component of modern sales strategies, enabling organizations to thrive in today's dynamic and highly competitive business environment.

Case Studies: Real-World Examples of Sales-Driven Growth

4.1 Case Study: Salesforce - Empowering Sales with Technology

Background: Salesforce, a global leader in customer relationship management (CRM) software, is a prime example of how technology can empower sales teams. The company's innovative CRM platform has revolutionized the way organizations manage customer relationships and drive sales growth.

Strategy: Salesforce empowers sales teams through a range of technological solutions:

1. Comprehensive CRM: Salesforce offers a comprehensive CRM platform that centralizes customer data, providing a 360-degree view of each prospect and customer. This enables sales professionals to personalize interactions and make data-driven decisions.

2. Automation: The platform automates repetitive tasks, such as data entry and lead routing, freeing up salespeople to focus on building relationships and closing deals.

3. Analytics: Salesforce provides robust analytics and reporting tools that offer insights into sales performance, customer behavior, and market trends. This data informs strategy and guides decision-making.

4. Collaboration: Salesforce facilitates collaboration across sales teams, ensuring seamless communication and knowledge sharing, regardless of geographic locations.

5. Personalization: With Salesforce's AI capabilities, sales teams can deliver personalized customer experiences, from tailored product recommendations to customized marketing campaigns.

Results: Salesforce's technology-driven approach to sales empowerment has yielded remarkable results:

Increased Productivity: Sales teams using Salesforce experience increased efficiency and productivity, as manual tasks are automated.

Improved Customer Relationships: The CRM platform enhances customer engagement, leading to stronger relationships and higher satisfaction.

Data-Driven Decisions: Salesforce's analytics empower sales leaders to make informed, data-driven decisions that drive revenue growth.

Scalability: The platform scales to meet the needs of businesses of all sizes, supporting their growth and expansion.

In conclusion, Salesforce's success in empowering sales with technology illustrates the transformative power of CRM and data-driven solutions in modern sales. By centralizing data, automating processes, and providing valuable insights, Salesforce enables sales teams to excel, drive revenue, and deliver exceptional customer experiences.

4.2 Case Study: Amazon - Expanding Markets and Customer-Centricity

Background: Amazon, the global e-commerce giant founded by Jeff Bezos, exemplifies a business strategy rooted in expanding markets and unwavering customer-centricity. Its relentless focus on these principles has fueled its remarkable growth.

Strategy: Amazon's approach revolves around two key strategies:

1. Market Expansion: Amazon has consistently sought to expand its presence across industries and geographies. It began as an online bookstore but rapidly diversified into selling a wide range of products, digital services, and cloud computing through Amazon Web Services (AWS). Its acquisition of Whole Foods marked its entry into the grocery sector. Amazon's innovation extends to developing proprietary technologies like Kindle, Echo, and Alexa, further broadening its market reach.

2. Customer-Centricity: Amazon prioritizes customer satisfaction above all else. The company's commitment to delivering value, convenience, and an exceptional customer experience is evident in its relentless pursuit of faster delivery times, user-friendly interfaces, and personalized recommendations.

Results: Amazon's dual focus on market expansion and customer-centricity has yielded impressive results:

Market Dominance: Amazon is a global leader in e-commerce, cloud computing, and digital streaming, enjoying a significant share of the market in multiple sectors.

Revenue Growth: Its relentless expansion has resulted in consistent revenue growth, making Amazon one of the most valuable companies worldwide.

Customer Trust: Amazon's customer-centric approach has earned the trust and loyalty of millions of customers, contributing to its continued success.

Innovation: Amazon's investments in technology and innovation have reshaped entire industries and set new standards for customer experience.

In conclusion, Amazon's case illustrates the power of expanding markets while remaining intensely customer-centric. By continuously seeking new opportunities and relentlessly improving the customer journey, Amazon has achieved remarkable growth and solidified its position as a global powerhouse.

4.3 Case Study: HubSpot - Inbound Marketing and Sales Synergy

Background: HubSpot, a renowned provider of inbound marketing and sales software, has successfully demonstrated the power of seamless synergy between inbound marketing and sales strategies. This synergy has transformed the way businesses attract, engage, and convert prospects into loyal customers.

Strategy: HubSpot's approach centers on the integration of inbound marketing and sales through its all-in-one platform:

1. Content-Driven Marketing: HubSpot employs inbound marketing techniques such as content creation, blogging, social media, and email marketing to attract and nurture leads. High-quality content provides value and solves pain points for prospects, positioning HubSpot as an industry authority.

2. Marketing Automation: HubSpot's platform includes marketing automation tools that nurture leads and guide them through the sales funnel. This ensures that leads are well-qualified before reaching the sales team.

3. CRM Integration: HubSpot's CRM seamlessly integrates with its marketing tools, enabling a unified view of customer interactions and behaviors. This empowers sales teams to engage leads and customers more effectively.

4. Sales Enablement: The platform provides sales teams with valuable insights, such as lead intelligence and email tracking, enhancing their ability to close deals.

Results: HubSpot's integration of inbound marketing and sales has yielded impressive results:

Lead Quality: The synergy ensures that sales teams receive well-qualified leads, increasing conversion rates and reducing wasted effort.

Efficiency: HubSpot streamlines marketing and sales processes, reducing manual tasks and enabling teams to focus on high-impact activities.

Revenue Growth: By nurturing leads and providing valuable insights to sales teams, HubSpot has contributed to consistent revenue growth for countless businesses.

Customer Satisfaction: The platform's customer-centric approach fosters satisfaction and loyalty among its user base.

In conclusion, HubSpot's case showcases the transformative potential of aligning inbound marketing and sales strategies. By seamlessly integrating these functions, businesses can streamline operations, improve lead quality, and drive revenue growth while delivering exceptional customer experiences.

Conclusion: The Symbiotic Relationship Between Sales and Growth

The interplay between sales and business growth is a dynamic and symbiotic relationship. Effective sales strategies, customer-centric approaches, and the measurement of sales effectiveness are all essential components of this relationship. By recognizing the critical role of sales in revenue generation, market expansion, and customer acquisition, organizations can position themselves for sustainable growth. Moreover, embracing a customer-centric culture and leveraging sales technology and analytics enable companies to adapt to evolving market dynamics and customer needs. In an ever-changing business landscape, mastering the interplay between sales and growth is the key to enduring success.

Part III: Spirituality
Chapter 11: Spirituality in the Workplace

The world of business is often associated with profit, competition, and performance metrics. However, a paradigm shift is occurring as more organizations recognize the value of spirituality in the workplace. In this chapter, we will explore the concept of spirituality in a business context, dissect its various dimensions, and delve into the profound benefits of infusing spirituality into business practices.

Defining Spirituality in Business

1.1 The Essence of Spirituality

The essence of spirituality in business lies in recognizing that commerce can be more than just profit-driven transactions; it can also be a force for positive change, personal growth, and collective well-being. Spirituality in business encompasses several key aspects:

Purpose and Meaning: Spiritual business leaders and organizations often prioritize a higher purpose beyond profits. They seek to make a positive impact on society, employees, and the environment.

Ethical Leadership: Spiritual business leaders prioritize ethical and compassionate leadership. They demonstrate empathy, fairness, and a commitment to the well-being of their employees and communities.

Work-Life Balance: Spirituality in business values the well-being and work-life balance of employees. It recognizes that a healthy and balanced workforce is more productive and fulfilled.

Sustainability: Spiritual businesses often adopt sustainable practices, recognizing the interconnectedness of all life and the importance of preserving the planet for future generations.

Mindfulness and Self-Awareness: Many spiritual approaches in business promote mindfulness, self-awareness, and personal growth, encouraging employees to find purpose and fulfillment in their work.

Community Engagement: Spiritual businesses actively engage with and contribute to their local and global communities, fostering a sense of social responsibility.

Ultimately, the essence of spirituality in business lies in recognizing that profit is just one dimension of success. True success encompasses holistic well-being, ethical conduct, and a commitment to making the world a better place, creating a harmonious and meaningful business environment for all involved.

1.2 Spirituality vs. Religion

Spirituality and religion are two related but distinct concepts that play significant roles in the lives of individuals and communities. Here's a brief comparison:

Spirituality:

Personal Journey: Spirituality is often a deeply personal and individualistic journey. It involves seeking a connection to something greater than oneself, which could be the universe, nature, or a sense of inner peace and purpose.

Flexibility: Spirituality is more flexible and adaptable than religion. It doesn't necessarily follow specific doctrines or organized rituals but instead focuses on personal growth, mindfulness, and inner exploration.

Inclusivity: Spirituality can encompass a wide range of beliefs and practices, making it more inclusive and open to diversity. It can coexist with various religious or non-religious backgrounds.

Religion:

Structured Belief System: Religion typically follows a structured belief system with established doctrines, rituals, and practices. It often involves organized institutions and religious texts.

Community and Tradition: Religion often fosters a sense of community and tradition. It provides a framework for shared beliefs, moral codes, and communal worship.

Specificity: Religions have specific deities, sacred texts, and doctrines that followers adhere to. They may have clear guidelines for behavior, worship, and salvation.

In summary, spirituality is a broader and more personal concept that can exist independently of organized religion. While spirituality emphasizes inner growth and connection to the transcendent, religion is often associated with specific beliefs, practices, and communal structures. Individuals may embrace one, the other, both, or neither, depending on their personal beliefs and experiences.

1.3 The Role of Spirituality in Business

Spirituality in business is about recognizing that employees are not just human resources but also individuals with inner lives, values, and aspirations. When integrated into business practices, spirituality can enhance organizational culture and well-being.

Spirituality's Role in Business:

Fostering a workplace culture of authenticity and purpose.

Encouraging ethical decision-making and social responsibility.

Supporting personal growth and holistic well-being.

Dimensions of Spirituality in Business

2.1 Purpose and Meaning

One dimension of spirituality in business is the pursuit of purpose and meaning in work. When employees see their work as contributing to a greater good, they are more motivated and engaged.

Cultivating Purpose and Meaning:

Aligning individual and organizational purpose.

Encouraging employees to find meaning in their roles.

Recognizing and celebrating the positive impact of work.

2.2 Ethics and Values

Ethical behavior and values alignment are central to spirituality in business. Organizations that prioritize ethical decision-making build trust with employees, customers, and stakeholders.

Nurturing Ethics and Values:

Developing a clear code of ethics and conduct.

Encouraging open discussions on ethical dilemmas.

Holding individuals and the organization accountable for ethical behavior.

2.3 Work-Life Balance

Balancing work and personal life is crucial for spiritual well-being. Organizations that support work-life balance foster healthier, more satisfied employees.

Supporting Work-Life Balance:

Offering flexible work arrangements.

Promoting stress management and mindfulness practices.

Recognizing the importance of holistic well-being beyond work.

Benefits of Infusing Spirituality into Business

3.1 Enhanced Employee Engagement

When employees find purpose and meaning in their work, they become more engaged and committed to their roles. Spirituality in business fosters a sense of belonging and fulfillment.

Impact on Employee Engagement:

Increased job satisfaction and motivation.

Higher levels of discretionary effort and innovation.

Reduced turnover and absenteeism.

3.2 Ethical Decision-Making

Infusing spirituality into business can lead to more ethical decision-making. Employees are more likely to make decisions aligned with their values when they feel supported in the workplace.

Promoting Ethical Decision-Making:

A stronger ethical culture within the organization.

Reduced instances of unethical behavior and misconduct.

Enhanced reputation and trust among stakeholders.

3.3 Improved Well-Being

Employees who experience a sense of balance between their work and personal lives report higher levels of well-being. Spirituality in business promotes holistic well-being.

Impact on Employee Well-Being:

Reduced stress and burnout.

Improved physical and mental health.

Greater overall life satisfaction.

3.4 Increased Innovation

A workplace that values spirituality often encourages open dialogue, diverse perspectives, and creative thinking. This, in turn, can lead to increased innovation and problem-solving.

Fostering Innovation:

A culture of openness to new ideas and experimentation.

Cross-functional collaboration and idea sharing.

A greater ability to adapt to changing market conditions.

3.5 Enhanced Customer and Stakeholder Relations

Organizations that prioritize spirituality often build stronger relationships with customers and stakeholders. Customers are drawn to businesses that align with their values, leading to greater loyalty.

Impact on Customer and Stakeholder Relations:

Increased customer loyalty and advocacy.

A positive brand image and reputation.

Enhanced partnerships and collaboration with stakeholders.

Implementing Spirituality in Business

4.1 Leadership Buy-In

Leaders play a crucial role in integrating spirituality into business practices. Their support and commitment set the tone for the entire organization.

Leadership's Role:

Modeling spiritual principles and values.

Incorporating spirituality into the organization's mission and vision.

Promoting a culture of authenticity and purpose.

4.2 Employee Training and Development

Organizations can provide training and development opportunities that foster spirituality in the workplace. These programs empower employees to find meaning in their roles and develop their ethical decision-making skills.

Spiritual Development Initiatives:

Offering mindfulness and well-being programs.

Providing ethics training and resources.

Encouraging self-awareness and personal growth.

4.3 Measurement and Assessment

To gauge the impact of spirituality in business, organizations can implement measurement and assessment tools to track key indicators of success.

Measuring Spirituality's Impact:

Surveys and feedback mechanisms to assess employee engagement and well-being.

Evaluating the ethical climate and instances of ethical decision-making.

Monitoring innovation and its impact on business outcomes.

Case Studies: Real-World Examples of Spirituality in Business

5.1 Patagonia - A Values-Driven Approach

Patagonia, the renowned outdoor clothing and gear company founded by Yvon Chouinard, is a compelling example of a values-driven approach that incorporates spirituality into its business ethos. The company's commitment to environmental and social responsibility is deeply ingrained in its corporate culture.

Values-Driven Approach: Patagonia's spirituality in business manifests through several core principles:

1. Environmental Stewardship: Patagonia places a high value on environmental sustainability. It actively supports and funds environmental causes, minimizes its environmental footprint, and encourages customers to buy less and make their clothing last longer.

2. Ethical Business Practices: The company prioritizes ethical manufacturing and fair labor practices. It's committed to fair wages, safe working conditions, and transparency in its supply chain.

3. Customer Engagement: Patagonia fosters a sense of community among its customers, encouraging them to align with its values. Its "Worn Wear" program promotes the idea that repairing and reusing clothing is an ethical choice.

4. Activism: Patagonia is not afraid to take a stand on environmental and social issues. It uses its platform to advocate for policies and actions that align with its values.

Results: Patagonia's values-driven approach has yielded impressive results:

Brand Loyalty: The company enjoys a fiercely loyal customer base that shares its values and appreciates its commitment to sustainability.

Positive Impact: Patagonia's contributions to environmental causes and ethical practices set an example for the industry and society at large.

Profitability: Despite its strong values, Patagonia remains a profitable business, demonstrating that values-driven approaches can be financially sustainable.

In conclusion, Patagonia's case exemplifies how a spirituality-based values-driven approach can lead to success in business. By aligning its operations with its core principles, the company has not only fostered brand loyalty but also made a significant positive impact on environmental and social issues, demonstrating the potential of business as a force for good in the world.

5.2 The Container Store - Employee-Centric Spirituality

The Container Store is a standout example of an organization that embodies employee-centric spirituality within its corporate culture. Founded by Kip Tindell, the company places a strong emphasis on nurturing a workplace environment where employees are not just workers but integral members of a close-knit community. Key elements of its employee-centric spirituality include:

1. Employee Empowerment: The Container Store believes in the intrinsic worth and potential of each employee. It empowers staff through training, development opportunities, and a collaborative atmosphere where their ideas and contributions are highly valued.

2. Conscious Capitalism: The company practices "conscious capitalism," emphasizing that business can and should be a force for good. This approach involves fair wages, generous benefits, and a strong commitment to community service.

3. Unconventional Management: The Container Store follows unconventional management practices, focusing on fostering employee well-being, happiness, and work-life balance. These practices enhance employee satisfaction and retention.

4. Exceptional Service: The company believes that happy employees lead to happy customers. Employee-centric spirituality translates into a dedicated, knowledgeable, and passionate workforce that delivers exceptional customer service.

5. Engaging Leadership: The Container Store's leadership team actively engages with employees and encourages open communication, creating a sense of belonging and shared purpose.

In conclusion, The Container Store exemplifies the concept of employee-centric spirituality, where the well-being, growth, and happiness of employees are at the core of its business philosophy. This approach has contributed to the company's success, demonstrating that a strong commitment to employees can lead to exceptional customer experiences and sustained business growth.

5.3 Google - Innovation and Creativity

Google stands as a beacon of innovation and creativity, showcasing how these qualities can be woven into the fabric of workplace spirituality. The company encourages employees to devote a portion of their work hours to personal projects, fostering a culture of creativity and autonomy. This approach has led to groundbreaking innovations like Gmail and Google Maps. Additionally, Google fosters a sense of purpose through its commitment to environmental sustainability and philanthropic initiatives. This spirit of innovation, creativity, and social responsibility not only attracts top talent but also infuses the workplace with a sense of higher purpose, exemplifying how spirituality can drive excellence in the tech industry.

Conclusion: The Transformational Power of Spirituality in Business

Infusing spirituality into business practices is a transformative journey that can lead to enhanced well-being, ethical decision-making, employee engagement, and innovation. By recognizing the importance of purpose, values, and work-life balance, organizations can create environments where individuals thrive and businesses flourish. The benefits extend beyond the workplace, positively impacting customers, stakeholders, and society at large. Embracing spirituality in business is not a departure from traditional practices but an evolution towards a more holistic and sustainable future.

Chapter 12: Belief, Trust, and Faith

In the realm of business, where strategies, data, and metrics often take the spotlight, there exists a profound and transformative force that goes beyond the numbers—the power of belief, trust, and faith. These spiritual concepts have a unique capacity to shape the culture, direction, and success of businesses. In this essay, we will explore the significance of belief, trust, and faith in the context of business, drawing inspiration from timeless spiritual texts that offer profound insights into how these principles can elevate and enrich business practices.

The Foundation of Belief

The Role of Belief in Business

Belief plays a profound role in business, influencing the actions, decisions, and overall culture within organizations. Here's how belief impacts various aspects of the business world:

Vision and Purpose: Belief provides the foundation for a company's vision and purpose. It's the driving force behind a business leader's determination to make a difference or solve a problem, and it guides the direction the company takes.

Leadership: Belief is a cornerstone of effective leadership. Leaders who believe in their mission inspire confidence and dedication in their teams, fostering a sense of unity and shared purpose.

Innovation: Belief in the possibility of improvement and progress fuels innovation. It encourages employees to think creatively, take risks, and explore new solutions.

Customer Trust: Belief in the value a product or service provides builds trust with customers. When businesses genuinely believe in the benefits they offer, it translates into more authentic marketing and customer relationships.

Culture: Belief shapes the organizational culture. Shared beliefs and values can create a positive workplace culture that attracts and retains talent.

Resilience: Belief helps businesses weather challenges and setbacks. When leaders and teams believe in their ability to overcome obstacles, they are more likely to persevere in the face of adversity.

Ethics: Belief in ethical principles guides businesses to make morally sound decisions and maintain integrity.

In conclusion, belief is a powerful force that underpins the vision, culture, and success of businesses. It drives innovation, fosters trust, and empowers leaders and employees to work towards a common purpose. Whether it's belief in a product, a mission, or a set of values, it is a driving force that propels businesses toward their goals.

The Power of Positive Thinking

The power of positive thinking in business cannot be overstated. It influences every facet of an organization's success, from leadership and employee morale to innovation and customer relationships. Here's why it's crucial:

Resilience: Positive thinking helps leaders and teams stay resilient in the face of challenges. It enables them to view setbacks as opportunities for growth and learning rather than insurmountable obstacles.

Problem-Solving: A positive mindset fosters creativity and problem-solving abilities. It encourages individuals to explore innovative solutions rather than dwelling on problems.

Motivation: Positive thinking fuels motivation and ambition. It inspires individuals to set and pursue ambitious goals, driving progress and achievement.

Team Dynamics: Teams with a positive atmosphere tend to collaborate better and support one another. This leads to improved communication, productivity, and overall job satisfaction.

Customer Relationships: Positive thinking influences how a business interacts with customers. It promotes a customer-centric approach, enhancing trust and satisfaction.

Leadership: Positive leaders are more effective in inspiring and guiding their teams. They create a culture of optimism that attracts and retains top talent.

In essence, positive thinking in business is not just a feel-good concept; it's a catalyst for growth, innovation, and overall success. It fosters a can-do attitude, resilience, and the belief that challenges can be overcome, making it an invaluable asset in the business world.

The Essence of Trust

Trust as a Cornerstone of Business

Trust is the cornerstone of business, underpinning every successful transaction and relationship. It's the bedrock on which partnerships, customer loyalty, and reputations are built. Businesses that prioritize trustworthiness inspire confidence and credibility, creating a competitive edge in a crowded marketplace. Trust enhances collaboration, fosters long-term customer relationships, and reduces friction in negotiations. It also attracts top talent and encourages employees to be more engaged and committed. Ultimately, trust isn't just a business asset; it's the currency of integrity and the foundation on which enduring success is constructed..

Trusting Intuition and Gut Feelings

Trusting intuition and gut feelings in business can be a powerful asset when balanced with data-driven decision-making. Intuition often draws on years of experience and a subconscious processing of information, helping business leaders make quick judgments in uncertain situations.

Innovation and entrepreneurial success are frequently born from gut instincts that defy conventional wisdom. Entrepreneurs like Steve Jobs relied heavily on intuition to guide their visionary endeavors.

However, intuition should be tempered by critical analysis and data. It's not infallible and can lead to errors in judgment if not kept in check. In situations where stakes are high, such as large investments or strategic decisions, empirical evidence and thorough research should complement intuition.

Ultimately, successful business leaders often find a harmony between gut feelings and data-driven decision-making. They recognize that both have their place in guiding the complex and dynamic world of business, creating a balanced approach that combines intuition with empirical evidence for the best possible outcomes.

The Strength of Faith

Faith in the Face of Uncertainty

Faith in the face of uncertainty is a testament to human resilience and determination. In business, where risks and challenges are constant companions, having faith can be a driving force for entrepreneurs and leaders.

This faith isn't necessarily religious; it's a belief in the potential for success, a commitment to a vision, and a willingness to persevere despite ambiguity. It's the unwavering conviction that, even when the path ahead is shrouded in uncertainty, one's efforts and decisions can lead to positive outcomes.

Faith in business is often tied to courage—the courage to take calculated risks, to innovate, and to face failure with resilience. It fuels creativity and entrepreneurship, encouraging individuals to pursue ideas that others might dismiss as too risky.

While faith alone can't guarantee success, it can be the catalyst that propels businesses forward in the face of doubt and adversity. It's a reminder that even amidst uncertainty, unwavering belief in one's abilities and goals can lead to remarkable achievements and breakthroughs.

Faith in Vision and Purpose

Faith in vision and purpose is the unwavering belief that a specific mission or goal holds profound meaning and significance. In the realm of business, this faith is the driving force behind entrepreneurial endeavors and organizational success.

A compelling vision, grounded in a strong sense of purpose, provides a roadmap for businesses. It instills a sense of direction, motivates employees, and aligns efforts toward a common goal. Faith in this vision and purpose fuels determination, resilience, and innovation. This faith is what enables entrepreneurs to persevere through challenges, setbacks, and uncertainty. It propels them to take risks, pursue bold ideas, and disrupt established norms. Likewise, for employees, faith in the organization's purpose fosters a sense of belonging and pride, inspiring them to work with passion and commitment.

In the business world, faith in vision and purpose is the cornerstone upon which great companies are built. It drives progress, inspires excellence, and creates a lasting impact on employees, customers, and society at large.

Insights from Spiritual Texts
The Bhagavad Gita: Finding Purpose and Belief

The Bhagavad Gita, a sacred text within Hinduism, offers profound insights on finding purpose and belief. It is a conversation between Prince Arjuna and Lord Krishna on the battlefield, and its teachings transcend time and culture.

The Gita teaches that purpose and belief are intertwined. It encourages individuals to align their actions with their innate dharma or life's purpose. By understanding and following one's dharma, individuals can find a deep sense of meaning and fulfillment.

Belief, according to the Gita, is rooted in faith in the divine order of the universe. It encourages individuals to have unwavering faith in their chosen path and to act with dedication and detachment from the outcomes.

The Gita emphasizes self-realization and the importance of inner peace as the foundation for finding one's purpose and living a purposeful life. It teaches that true belief arises from self-awareness, inner clarity, and a profound connection with the divine.

In essence, the Bhagavad Gita offers timeless wisdom on the interplay between belief and purpose, guiding individuals on a path towards a life filled with meaning, purpose, and spiritual fulfillment.

The Bible: Trusting in Divine Guidance

The Bible offers valuable insights on trusting in divine guidance in business, highlighting the significance of faith, wisdom, and ethical conduct. Here are key principles:

Proverbs 3:5-6: "Trust in the LORD with all your heart and lean not on your own understanding; in all your ways submit to him, and he will make your paths straight." This passage underscores the importance of seeking divine wisdom and guidance in all aspects of life, including business. Trusting in God's direction can lead to sound decision-making and righteous paths.

Ethical Business Practices: The Bible emphasizes honesty, integrity, and fair dealings in business. Proverbs 11:1 states, "The LORD detests dishonest scales, but accurate weights find favor with him." Trust in divine guidance extends to conducting business with integrity and treating others justly.

Seeking God's Will: James 4:13-15 encourages businesspeople to seek God's will in their plans: "Now listen, you who say, 'Today or tomorrow we will go to this or that city, spend a year there, carry on business and make money.'... Instead, you ought to say, 'If it is the Lord's will, we will live and do this or that.'" It emphasizes the importance of humility and recognizing that God's guidance should shape business endeavors.

Prioritizing People: The Bible places emphasis on relationships and valuing people over profits. Matthew 22:39 teaches to "love your neighbor as yourself." In business, this translates to treating employees, customers, and stakeholders with respect and compassion.

Incorporating these biblical principles into business practices can lead to a harmonious, ethical, and purpose-driven approach to entrepreneurship and leadership. Trusting in divine guidance not only supports ethical decision-making but also fosters a sense of accountability and purpose in the business world.

The Tao Te Ching: Embracing the Flow of Business

The Tao Te Ching, a foundational text in Taoism written by Lao Tzu, offers profound insights on embracing the flow of business. It emphasizes the concept of "Tao," often translated as "the Way," which encourages individuals to align with the natural order of things rather than resist it.

In the context of business, the Tao Te Ching teaches that success comes not from forceful control or rigid strategies but from embracing the natural flow of opportunities and challenges. It encourages leaders to adopt a more flexible and adaptive approach, similar to the way water flows around obstacles.

The text also emphasizes the importance of humility and simplicity in business dealings. It suggests that business leaders should not seek excessive power or material wealth but should instead focus on ethical conduct, harmonious relationships, and providing value to others.

Furthermore, the Tao Te Ching promotes the idea of "Wu Wei," often translated as "effortless action" or "non-action." This concept encourages individuals to act in alignment with the Tao, exerting minimal force and allowing things to unfold naturally.

In essence, the Tao Te Ching offers a timeless wisdom that encourages business leaders to flow with the currents of change, to be adaptable and humble, and to seek harmony and balance in their business endeavors. It teaches that by embracing the flow of business, individuals can achieve sustainable success while maintaining a sense of inner peace and integrity.

Practical Application in Business
Cultivating Belief, Trust, and Faith

Practical strategies for nurturing belief, trust, and faith within the business environment, encompassing leadership practices, employee engagement, and organizational culture.

Cultivating Spiritual Principles:

Cultivating spiritual principles involves nurturing qualities like compassion, mindfulness, gratitude, and empathy. It's about aligning one's actions with higher values, seeking inner growth, and fostering a sense of interconnectedness with all life. These principles guide ethical decision-making, promote personal well-being, and enhance relationships, whether in personal life or business. By cultivating spiritual principles, individuals and organizations can create a more harmonious, compassionate, and purpose-driven environment, leading to greater fulfillment and positive impact on the world around them.

Ethical Business Practices

Ethical business practices and ethical decision-making are foundational to maintaining integrity, trust, and sustainability in the business world. Ethical business practices encompass a set of values and principles that guide an organization's behavior and interactions with stakeholders.

Transparency: Ethical businesses prioritize transparency in their operations, openly sharing information with stakeholders, including employees, customers, and investors. This transparency builds trust and accountability.

Fairness: Ethical decision-making involves treating all individuals and groups fairly and equitably. This includes ensuring fair wages, nondiscriminatory hiring practices, and ethical procurement.

Social Responsibility: Ethical businesses recognize their role in the broader community and environment. They strive to minimize negative impacts and contribute positively through philanthropy, sustainable practices, and community engagement.

Integrity: Ethical decision-making prioritizes honesty and integrity in all dealings. This includes refraining from deceptive marketing, insider trading, and other unethical practices.

Compliance: Ethical businesses adhere to all relevant laws and regulations, ensuring that their operations are both legal and ethical.

Accountability: Ethical practices involve holding individuals and organizations accountable for their actions. This often means acknowledging mistakes, rectifying them, and learning from them.

Ultimately, ethical business practices and decision-making contribute to long-term success. They build a positive reputation, foster trust among stakeholders, and create a workplace culture that attracts and retains talent. Ethical businesses not only aim for profitability but also prioritize their impact on society, striving to make the world a better place through their actions.

Case Studies: Real-World Examples

Patagonia: Belief in Environmental Responsibility

Patagonia, the renowned outdoor clothing and gear company founded by Yvon Chouinard, is a compelling case study of a business that exemplifies unwavering belief in environmental responsibility. This belief is deeply ingrained in the company's culture and operations.

Environmental Responsibility: Patagonia's commitment to environmental responsibility is evident through several key initiatives:

1. Sustainability: Patagonia prioritizes sustainability at every stage of its products' lifecycle, from design and sourcing materials to manufacturing and customer use. The company continually seeks ways to reduce its environmental footprint.

2. Activism: Patagonia is not just a clothing brand; it's also an advocate for the environment. The company has launched campaigns, such as "Don't Buy This Jacket," encouraging customers to reduce consumption and support environmental causes.

3. Environmental Grants: Through its "1% for the Planet" program, Patagonia donates a percentage of its sales to grassroots environmental organizations worldwide, contributing millions of dollars to date.

4. Repair and Reuse: Patagonia promotes repairing and reusing its products through its "Worn Wear" program, encouraging customers to extend the lifespan of their clothing.

Results: Patagonia's unwavering belief in environmental responsibility has yielded impressive results:

Brand Loyalty: The company enjoys a fiercely loyal customer base that shares its values and appreciates its commitment to sustainability.

Positive Impact: Patagonia's contributions to environmental causes and sustainable practices set an example for the industry and society at large.

Profitability: Despite its strong values, Patagonia remains a profitable business, demonstrating that environmental responsibility can be financially sustainable.

In conclusion, Patagonia's case showcases the transformative potential of embracing environmental responsibility as a core belief. By integrating sustainability, activism, and ethical practices, the company has not only fostered brand loyalty but also made a significant positive impact on environmental issues, demonstrating that business can be a force for good in the world.

Zappos: Trusting in Company Culture

Zappos, an online shoe and clothing retailer, serves as a prime example of an organization that places immense trust in its company culture. Founded by Tony Hsieh, Zappos has cultivated a unique culture built on values like customer service, employee empowerment, and a fun, quirky atmosphere.

This trust in company culture is evident through practices like offering employees monetary incentives to leave if they feel the company isn't a good fit. Zappos believes that employees who resonate with their culture are more likely to deliver exceptional customer service.

This unconventional approach has paid off, fostering a loyal workforce and earning Zappos a reputation for exceptional customer service. It demonstrates that trust in a well-defined and nurtured company culture can drive success and set a remarkable standard in the retail industry.

Tesla: Faith in Innovation

Tesla, led by visionary entrepreneur Elon Musk, stands as an exemplary embodiment of faith in innovation. The company's core belief revolves around the transformative potential of electric vehicles (EVs) and sustainable energy solutions.

Tesla's unwavering faith in innovation is evident through several key facets:

Cutting-Edge Technology: Tesla consistently pushes the boundaries of EV technology, striving to make electric vehicles not only practical but also exciting. Their commitment to innovation has led to advancements in battery technology, autonomous driving, and energy storage.

Sustainable Vision: Tesla's mission to accelerate the world's transition to sustainable energy is rooted in a deep belief in the positive impact of renewable energy sources on the environment. They invest in solar energy, energy storage, and EVs as part of this vision.

Market Leadership: Tesla's success in becoming one of the world's most valuable automakers is a testament to its faith in innovation. They've shown that EVs can compete with and surpass traditional gasoline-powered vehicles in terms of performance and market appeal.

Risky Ventures: Tesla's willingness to take risks, from building the Gigafactories to launching ambitious vehicle projects like the Cybertruck, reflects its faith in pioneering technologies and disrupting traditional industries.

In conclusion, Tesla's remarkable journey illustrates how faith in innovation can redefine industries and inspire global movements toward a more sustainable and technologically advanced future. It demonstrates that believing in the transformative power of innovation can yield unprecedented success and influence positive change on a global scale.

Conclusion

The power of belief, trust, and faith is a profound force that transcends the boundaries of conventional business practices. Drawing inspiration from timeless spiritual texts, we have explored how these principles can elevate, enrich, and transform business endeavors. As individuals and organizations embrace these principles, they not only find deeper fulfillment in their work but also contribute to a more compassionate, purpose-driven, and harmonious world of business. In the intricate dance of belief, trust, and faith, businesses can find the resilience to weather storms, the inspiration to innovate, and the integrity to thrive while upholding their values.

Chapter 13: Mindfulness and Well-being

In today's fast-paced and competitive world, the practice of mindfulness has emerged as a profound force of change. This chapter delves into the deep impact of mindfulness in leadership, sales, and workplace well-being, highlighting its transformative power and how it has disrupted conventional paradigms. We will explore real-world examples and case studies that illuminate the profound shifts brought about by mindfulness in these critical domains.

Mindfulness: A Path to Inner Transformation

At its core, mindfulness is the practice of being fully present in the moment, with open awareness and without judgment. It is rooted in ancient wisdom and has found its way into modern leadership and business practices.

Mindful leaders like Satya Nadella, the CEO of Microsoft, have embraced this practice to foster a new paradigm of leadership. Nadella's emphasis on empathy, self-awareness, and ethical decision-making has redefined the role of leadership. By encouraging mindfulness practices such as meditation and self-reflection, he has created an inclusive and innovative corporate culture.

Mindful Selling: A Shift in Perspective

Sales, traditionally associated with aggressive tactics and targets, is undergoing a significant transformation through mindfulness. Mindful selling emphasizes authenticity, empathy, and building genuine connections with customers.

An example of mindful selling can be seen at Zappos, the online retailer. Under the leadership of Tony Hsieh, Zappos redefined its sales approach. Mindful selling prioritized customer relationships over quick sales, with sales representatives practicing mindfulness techniques to listen actively and empathize with customers. This approach not only increased customer satisfaction but also boosted sales figures, demonstrating the profitability of ethical and empathetic selling.

Well-being in the Workplace: A Holistic Approach

In an era marked by stress and burnout, organizations are recognizing the importance of prioritizing employee well-being. Mindfulness plays a central role in creating a healthy workplace culture. Google, a pioneer in workplace well-being, offers mindfulness programs to its employees. Through meditation and mindfulness classes, employees are encouraged to prioritize self-care. This has led to lower stress levels, increased job satisfaction, and greater productivity among Google's workforce. It is a testament to how mindfulness can create a workplace where employees not only perform well but also feel supported and valued.

Resilience in Times of Change

The integration of mindfulness in leadership, sales, and well-being practices is not just a trend; it's a revolution. Mindfulness equips individuals and organizations with the resilience to navigate the complexities and uncertainties of the modern world.

In the face of challenges, Jon Kabat-Zinn's Mindfulness-Based Stress Reduction (MBSR) program has been transformative for individuals and organizations alike. It has been adopted by companies such as General Mills and Aetna to enhance employee well-being and resilience. By teaching employees to manage stress through mindfulness, these organizations have experienced reduced healthcare costs, increased employee retention, and improved overall productivity.

Conclusion: A Mindful Revolution

In conclusion, the practice of mindfulness has ushered in a mindful revolution that is reshaping leadership, sales, and workplace well-being. Leaders like Satya Nadella, organizations like Zappos and Google, and programs like MBSR exemplify the profound impact of mindfulness. It is not just a tool for success; it is a catalyst for profound transformation, fostering a future where mindfulness is integral to conscious, compassionate, and successful living.

Part IV: The Harmony of Leadership, Sales, and Spirituality

Chapter 14: Creating a Successful Business

In the ever-evolving landscape of business, the quest for success has evolved beyond mere financial prosperity. Today, organizations are increasingly recognizing the profound potential of integrating leadership, sales, and spirituality as a holistic approach to achieving not only profitability but also enduring and meaningful success. In this chapter, we will delve into this transformative integration and explore how real-world businesses have harnessed the synergy of these elements to attain remarkable success.

Leadership: A Beacon of Wisdom

At the heart of the triad lies leadership, the guiding force that steers organizations toward their objectives. Leadership, however, is evolving beyond traditional models. It is increasingly seen as a practice rooted in mindfulness and authenticity.

One compelling example of this mindful leadership is Google. This tech giant, led by figures like Sundar Pichai, has embraced a leadership philosophy deeply rooted in mindfulness. Google understands that effective leaders must be self-aware, empathetic, and in tune with the well-being of their teams. Through mindfulness practices such as meditation and mindfulness-based leadership training, Google fosters an environment where employees feel valued, respected, and inspired. The result is a culture of innovation, creativity, and high performance.

Sales: The Art of Authentic Connection

Sales, often seen as a numbers game, is undergoing a transformation. Businesses are realizing that authentic connections with customers are more valuable than quick transactions. Sales, in this context, becomes a mindful practice driven by empathy and ethical values.

One exemplar of mindful sales is Patagonia, the renowned outdoor clothing company. Patagonia's sales strategy is not solely about selling products but also about fostering a deeper connection with its customers. The company encourages sustainability, ethical sourcing, and environmentally responsible practices. By aligning their sales practices with their customers' values and concerns, Patagonia builds trust and loyalty. Their commitment to transparency and their pledge to donate a significant portion of profits to environmental causes resonate with customers who seek products with a purpose.

Spirituality: The Foundation of Values

Spirituality, often viewed as a personal domain, is increasingly finding its place in the corporate world. It provides the moral compass that guides businesses toward ethical and sustainable practices.

The Body Shop is an exemplary business that embodies spirituality in its core values. Founded by Anita Roddick, The Body Shop has consistently championed ethical practices, sustainability, and social responsibility. Roddick's spiritual values were woven into the company's DNA from the beginning. The Body Shop's commitment to fair trade, cruelty-free products, and environmental stewardship is a testament to how spirituality can drive ethical business practices. The company's success is not just measured in profits but in the positive impact it has on the world.

Conclusion: The Triad as a Blueprint for Success

The integration of leadership, sales, and spirituality represents a profound blueprint for success in the contemporary business landscape. The real-world examples of Google, Patagonia, and The Body Shop illustrate that these principles are not mere theories but practical strategies. By embracing this triad, organizations can navigate the complexities of the business world while fostering a culture of wisdom, authenticity, and ethical excellence. This integration isn't a trend but a transformative approach to achieving meaningful and enduring success.

◇

Chapter 15: The Path Forward

At the heart of this blueprint is the triad of leadership, sales, and spirituality. These three elements are interconnected, with each component reinforcing the others. Let's begin by understanding their individual significance before exploring their synergistic potential.

Leadership: The Compass for Growth

Leadership is the foundation upon which any successful business is built. Effective leaders set the vision, steer the ship, and inspire their teams to achieve greatness. However, in the context of continuous growth, leadership must evolve.

Leadership in this triad is not about authority and hierarchy but about fostering a culture of empathy, self-awareness, and ethical decision-making. Leaders who practice mindfulness and spirituality are better equipped to navigate the complexities of the business world. They lead by example, encouraging their teams to embrace mindfulness practices, such as meditation and self-reflection.

Sales: Building Authentic Relationships

Sales are the lifeblood of any business. However, the traditional approach to sales often focuses on quotas, closing deals, and maximizing profits. In the triad, sales undergoes a transformation.

Mindful sales prioritize authenticity, empathy, and building genuine connections with customers. Salespeople are encouraged to practice mindfulness, allowing them to listen actively and empathize with clients. Instead of pushing for quick transactions, the focus is on understanding customers' needs and values.

Spirituality: The Ethical Compass

Spirituality, often seen as a personal domain, has a profound impact on business ethics and values. In the triad, spirituality provides the ethical compass that guides businesses toward responsible and sustainable practices.

Organizations that embrace spirituality often place a strong emphasis on ethical decision-making, social responsibility, and sustainability. Spirituality in this context is not tied to a particular religion but encompasses values such as compassion, integrity, and a commitment to the greater good.

The Blueprint for Implementation

Now that we have a deeper understanding of each component of the triad, let's explore the blueprint for implementing this holistic approach to continuous growth and success in business.

1. Leadership Development

Identify existing leaders who align with the principles of mindful and spiritual leadership.

Provide leadership training that emphasizes self-awareness, empathy, and ethical decision-making.

Encourage leaders to establish a personal mindfulness practice and lead by example.

Create opportunities for leaders to mentor and guide their teams in mindfulness and self-reflection.

2. Sales Transformation

Shift the sales culture from a transactional approach to one focused on building relationships.

Integrate mindfulness training into sales programs to enhance active listening and empathy.

Encourage sales teams to understand and align with customers' values and needs.

Reward sales representatives not only for revenue generation but also for fostering customer loyalty and trust.

3. Fostering a Spiritually Grounded Culture

Promote ethical values and social responsibility throughout the organization.

Develop a code of conduct that reflects the organization's commitment to spirituality and ethical behavior.

Establish sustainability initiatives that align with the organization's values and mission.

Encourage employees to volunteer and engage in community service as a way of living the organization's spiritual values.

4. Continuous Growth Monitoring

Regularly assess the impact of the triad on leadership effectiveness, sales performance, and the organizational culture.

Collect feedback from employees and customers to gauge the authenticity of relationships and ethical practices.

Adjust the implementation blueprint based on feedback and changing market dynamics.

Celebrate and acknowledge successes and milestones achieved through the triad's integration.

5. Long-Term Sustainability

Recognize that the integration of leadership, sales, and spirituality is not a short-term strategy but a long-term commitment.

Continuously reinforce the organization's commitment to its values and principles.

Foster a culture of adaptability and learning, embracing change as an opportunity for growth.

Encourage employees at all levels to embody the triad's principles, creating a cohesive and values-driven organization.

Conclusion: The Triad as a Path to Continuous Growth

In conclusion, the blueprint for implementing the triad of leadership, sales, and spirituality provides a holistic approach to sustaining success through continuous growth. By recognizing the interconnectedness of these elements and embracing their transformative potential, organizations can not only thrive in the short term but also create a lasting legacy of ethical, empathetic, and sustainable business practices. The triad is not a fixed destination but a journey toward continuous growth and enduring success in the ever-changing landscape of business.

Conclusion
Reflecting on the Transformative Journey

The Endless Possibilities of a Balanced Business As we conclude our exploration of the transformative journey of the triad—leadership, sales, and spirituality—in the context of business, we stand at the threshold of a new paradigm. Throughout this journey, we've delved deep into the individual components of this triad, witnessed their synergistic potential, and explored real-world examples of businesses that have embraced this holistic approach. In this conclusion, we reflect on the profound transformations and endless possibilities that emerge from the integration of these elements, paving the way for balanced and sustainable business practices.

The Triad: A Journey of Integration

The triad of leadership, sales, and spirituality represents a radical shift in the way businesses operate. It's a journey of integration, where traditional silos and hierarchical structures give way to a more holistic and values-driven approach. Let's reflect on the key takeaways from each component of the triad:

Leadership: Mindful leadership has emerged as the cornerstone of wisdom in the business world. Leaders who embrace self-awareness, empathy, and ethical decision-making create environments where employees thrive. Case studies like Satya Nadella at Microsoft have shown us that leadership can be a force for positive change, fostering innovation and inclusivity.

Sales: The transformation of sales from a transactional approach to one focused on building authentic relationships has redefined success. Mindful selling emphasizes empathy, active listening, and aligning with customer values. Examples like Zappos and its customer-centric philosophy highlight the profitability of ethical and empathetic sales practices.

Spirituality: Spirituality provides the moral compass that guides businesses toward ethical and sustainable practices. Organizations that embrace spirituality prioritize social responsibility, ethical decision-making, and sustainability. The Body Shop's commitment to ethical business practices illustrates the profound impact of spirituality in shaping an organization's values.

The Synergy of the Triad: Transforming Business Culture

When these three components converge, the synergy is transformative. Mindful leaders who embrace spirituality foster cultures of authenticity, compassion, and ethical excellence. Sales teams that practice empathy and active listening build trust and loyalty, ultimately driving business growth. Ethical values rooted in spirituality permeate the organizational culture, creating a workplace where employees feel supported, valued, and fulfilled.

The Endless Possibilities of a Balanced Business

As we reflect on the transformative journey of the triad, we are met with a profound realization: the possibilities are endless for businesses that embrace this holistic approach. Let's explore some of the key possibilities:

1. Sustainable Profitability: Businesses that prioritize mindful leadership and ethical sales practices are not only profitable in the short term but also create a foundation for sustainable growth. Customers are drawn to organizations that align with their values, resulting in long-term loyalty and increased revenue.

2. Innovation and Creativity: Mindful leadership fosters environments where innovation and creativity thrive. Employees are empowered to bring their authentic selves to work, leading to fresh ideas and groundbreaking solutions.

3. Employee Well-being: Organizations that prioritize spirituality and employee well-being experience reduced turnover, higher job satisfaction, and improved productivity. A workplace that values its employees as whole individuals creates a positive feedback loop of success.

4. Ethical and Social Responsibility: By integrating spirituality into business practices, organizations become champions of ethical and social responsibility. They contribute positively to their communities, minimize their environmental impact, and serve as ethical role models in their industries.

5. Adaptability and Resilience: Balanced businesses are better equipped to navigate the complexities and uncertainties of the modern world. Mindful leaders and employees who embrace spirituality are more adaptable and resilient in the face of change.

Conclusion: A New Horizon of Business Possibilities

In conclusion, the transformative journey of the triad—leadership, sales, and spirituality—offers a new horizon of endless possibilities for businesses. This holistic approach challenges conventional notions of success and paves the way for balanced, ethical, and sustainable business practices. Real-world examples, such as Google, Zappos, and The Body Shop, demonstrate that this journey is not a theoretical concept but a practical strategy for achieving enduring success.

As businesses continue to evolve, the triad stands as a guiding principle, creating a future where organizations are not only profit-driven but also values-driven. The possibilities are boundless for businesses that embark on this transformative journey, fostering a world of conscious, compassionate, and successful enterprises. The triad is not the end; it's the beginning of a new era in business—a journey of integration, transformation, and endless possibilities.

Seeds from the Author:

1. *Make your decisions in such a way today, that you can decide again tomorrow and tomorrow is not decided for you*
2. *For the believer their time on earth is the only Hell they will ever know. For the unbeliever their time on earth is the only*

Heaven they will ever know.

Appendices

Here is a list of additional resources and recommended readings for further learning on the topics of leadership, sales, spirituality, and their integration for a successful business:

Leadership:

"Leaders Eat Last: Why Some Teams Pull Together and Others Don't" by Simon Sinek - This book explores the concept of leadership from a perspective of trust, empathy, and creating a strong sense of purpose within organizations.

"Daring Greatly: How the Courage to Be Vulnerable Transforms the Way We Live, Love, Parent, and Lead" by Brené Brown - Brené Brown's work on vulnerability and authentic leadership has resonated with many. This book delves into the power of vulnerability in leadership.

"The Mindful Leader: Awakening Your Natural Management Skills Through Mindfulness Meditation" by Michael Carroll - Michael Carroll discusses how mindfulness can be applied to leadership to create more compassionate and effective leaders.

Sales:

"To Sell Is Human: The Surprising Truth About Moving Others" by Daniel H. Pink - Daniel Pink explores the changing nature of sales and how persuasion and influence are critical skills in various aspects of life, including sales.

"SPIN Selling" by Neil Rackham - A classic in the field of sales, this book introduces the SPIN (Situation, Problem, Implication, Need-payoff) technique for effective selling.

"The Challenger Sale: Taking Control of the Customer Conversation" by Matthew Dixon and Brent Adamson - This book presents a research-based approach to sales, emphasizing the value of challenging customers' preconceptions.

Spirituality:

"The Power of Now: A Guide to Spiritual Enlightenment" by Eckhart Tolle - Eckhart Tolle's work on spirituality and mindfulness has had a profound impact. "The Power of Now" explores the concept of living in the present moment.

"A New Earth: Awakening to Your Life's Purpose" by Eckhart Tolle - Another insightful book by Eckhart Tolle, this work delves into the transformational potential of spiritual awakening.

"The Seven Spiritual Laws of Success: A Practical Guide to the Fulfillment of Your Dreams" by Deepak Chopra - Deepak Chopra presents seven principles that can lead to spiritual and material success.

Integration of Leadership, Sales, and Spirituality:

"The 7 Habits of Highly Effective People: Powerful Lessons in Personal Change" by Stephen R. Covey - While not explicitly about the triad, this classic book covers principles of leadership, personal effectiveness, and ethics that align with the integration of leadership, sales, and spirituality.

"Conscious Capitalism: Liberating the Heroic Spirit of Business" by John Mackey and Raj Sisodia - This book explores how businesses can embrace conscious practices, aligning with the values of leadership, sales, and spirituality.

"The Mindful Marketer: How to Stay Present and Profitable in a Data-Driven World" by Lisa Nirell - This book combines mindfulness with marketing, emphasizing the importance of authenticity and ethical marketing practices.

These resources offer a rich and diverse set of perspectives on leadership, sales, spirituality, and their integration into a successful business model. Whether you're looking to enhance your leadership skills, improve your sales techniques, explore spirituality, or integrate these elements into your business strategy, these books provide valuable insights and guidance.

Acknowledgements:

I would like to begin this acknowledgement with heartfelt gratitude to my Heavenly Father, whose unwavering guidance and blessings have illuminated my path throughout the journey of writing this book. Your divine presence has been my constant source of strength and inspiration.

To my beloved wife, Chanelle, and my cherished children, your unwavering support, patience, and understanding have been the pillars upon which I built this endeavor. Your love fuels my determination and fills every page with purpose.

To my parents Manie and Jannet that always believed in me and taught me about values and integrity, you were the Northstar that set the course of my life and career. I am grateful for my mother-in-law, Mirna, who came into my life and taught me about hard work and family values and never giving up and to keep on having faith even when things don't go according to plan.

I am indebted to the remarkable leaders of the companies I've had the privilege to work for. Stephen from Waco International, Mark, Craig, Nabeel, and Sean from Absto – your wisdom, mentorship, and the opportunities you've provided have shaped me into the person I am today. Your belief in my potential has been a driving force.

Lastly, I extend my deepest appreciation to Natalie from One Ninety Consulting. Over the past year and a half, your coaching has been transformative. Your lessons on self-mastery have taught me that the answers lie within myself, and I am eternally grateful for the growth and enlightenment you've facilitated.

This book is a culmination of the invaluable contributions and support from these exceptional individuals and the divine guidance of my Heavenly Father. I am truly blessed to have you all in my life, and I dedicate this work to each one of you.

About the Author:

Jan Kriel's life has been a journey defined by education, family, career, and a commitment to personal growth. Born and raised in South Africa, his early years laid the foundation for a life of purpose and achievement.

In 1996, Jan Kriel proudly graduated from Secunda High School, marking the end of one chapter and the beginning of another. Armed with his matriculation, he embarked on an academic adventure that would further shape his future. His path led him to the esteemed University of Pretoria, where he pursued higher education. The university not only expanded his knowledge but also broadened his horizons, exposing him to diverse cultures, ideas, and perspectives.

In the realm of personal life, Jan Kriel's narrative took a beautiful turn when he entered the sacred institution of marriage. With the love and support of his life partner, he embraced the role of a devoted husband and father to six wonderful children. Family became the heart of his story, filling it with love, joy, and purpose.

Professionally, Jan Kriel ventured into the dynamic worlds of management and sales. Over the course of more than 18 years, he navigated the intricacies of these roles, combining his strong work ethic with a knack for connecting with people. His career was marked by achievements that reflected his dedication to personal growth and excellence.

Jan Kriel's thirst for knowledge and professional development led him to complete various leadership courses. These educational pursuits sharpened his leadership skills, honed his decision-making abilities, and equipped him to tackle the challenges of leadership roles with confidence and resilience.

Throughout his autobiography, Jan Kriel's life serves as a testament to the power of education, family, and perseverance. His journey illustrates the profound impact of a solid educational foundation, the joys of a loving family, and the rewards of a successful career marked by continuous growth and learning. As he continues to write the chapters of his life, Jan Kriel's story stands as an inspiration to those who aspire to create a life defined by purpose, achievement, and personal development.

Copyright

Page

Did you love *Leadership, Sales and Spirituality: A Harmonious Blueprint for Business Success*? Then you should read *Apocalypse Unveiled: Exploring Biblical End Time Prophecies*[1] by Jan Jacobus Kriel!

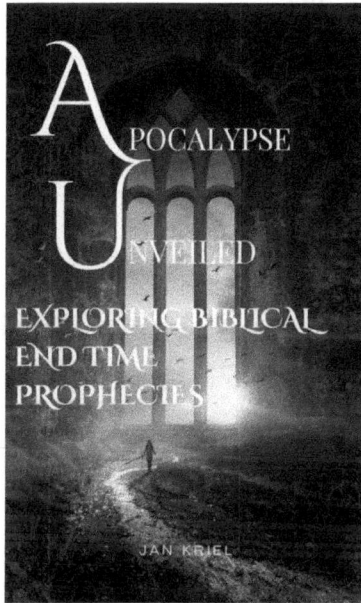

In a world filled with uncertainty and rapid change, the fascination with end time prophecies has never waned. "Apocalypse Unveiled" offers an insightful and scholarly examination of the most significant prophecies found in the Bible. Through a meticulous analysis of texts from both the Old and New Testaments, this book deciphers the hidden meanings behind these prophetic verses.

Apocalypse Unveiled" is a balanced and scholarly work that welcomes readers of all backgrounds, from the devoutly religious to the academically curious. It seeks to provide a nuanced exploration

1. https://books2read.com/u/4XEoX5

2. https://books2read.com/u/4XEoX5

of end time prophecies, encouraging readers to consider the spiritual, psychological, and social implications of these age-old predictions.

In a world where uncertainty and anxiety often prevail, this book will empower readers to engage with the biblical end time prophecies in a meaningful way and find hope, guidance, and inspiration in the face of an uncertain future.

www.ingramcontent.com/pod-product-compliance
Lightning Source LLC
Chambersburg PA
CBHW071837200326
41519CB00016B/4138